Puffin Books

Editor: Kaye Webb

THE PUFFIN BOOK

Modern football began in England less than 100
years ago, but 800 million people all over the
world watched the World Cup Final in Mexico
on television in 1970. That competition was a
triumph for spectacular, attacking football, full of
goals, personalities and excitement – the qualities
that have made football the world's most popular
spectator sport and the game of children in Rio de
Janeiro, Milan, Moscow, Glasgow and London.

Brian Glanville's book gives a clear, objective
account of how soccer came to be what it is today;
how a game which grew up in the English Public
Schools has been brought to Europe, America,
Africa and Asia. It describes, simply and
understandably, with diagrams and pictures, the
growth of tactics, from the old five-forward game,
through the third-back formation to the 4-2-4, 4-4-3
and sweeper systems of today. We follow the
development of English club football as well as the
history of the World Cup.

Much attention is given to the star names and
teams. To Steve Bloomer, Charlie Buchan, Dixie
Dean, Stanley Matthews and Alex James, from the
days when footballers earned a few pounds a week
and wore shorts to their knees; to Tom Finney and
Billy Wright, Puskas and his great Hungarians,
Di Stefano and the immaculate Real Madrid team
of the 1950s and 1960s; to the great stars of
the present, wealthy young heroes like Pelé,
Jairzinho, Riva, Best, Beckenbauer and Moore.

Every boy who reads *The Puffin Book of Football*
should derive a deeper interest in and understanding of
the game; of how it has developed, what it has become,
and what may or may not happen to it in the future.

Cover design by Peter Barrett

The Puffin Book of Football

Brian Glanville

Illustrated by Helen Fisher

Puffin Books

Puffin Books: a Division of Penguins Books Ltd
Harmondsworth, Middlesex, England
Penguin Books Inc., 7110 Ambassador Road,
Baltimore, Maryland 21207, U.S.A.
Penguin Books Australia Ltd, Ringwood,
Victoria, Australia

First published 1970
Reissued (with a Postscript) 1971
Reprinted 1972 (twice), 1973
Copyright © Brian Glanville, 1970, 1971, 1972
Illustrations copyright © Helen Fisher, 1970

Made and printed in Great Britain by
Hazell Watson & Viney Ltd
Aylesbury, Bucks
Set in Linotype Times

To Mark, Toby and Peregrine

Contents

1. Beginnings

Soccer, Association Football, has conquered the world: if one excepts North America. The game which developed late last century, in the English public schools and universities, is now played with passionate enthusiasm from Rio to Rangoon, from Iceland to Algeria. The great stars may come from poor Negro families in the interior of Brazil, like Pelé, or from the sombre back-streets of Belfast, like George Best. In Italy, the game is so popular that the crowd which watched Milan beat Manchester United in the semi-final of the European Cup of 1968–9 paid over £150,000, while to buy the transfer of a leading player, a club would have to pay twice as much. In Russia, important matches attract 100,000 spectators to the Lenin Stadium, in Moscow; 120,000 pack the Bernabeu Stadium, in Spain, when Real Madrid play a vital European Cup-tie.

The World Cup, initiated in 1930, has now grown by

such leaps and bounds that Asian and African qualifying zones have had to be added to those long since established in Europe, South America and Central America; and the original entry consists of more than seventy countries.

Far from being hurt by the growth and power of television, football has taken it in its stride; has used it, indeed, to become more popular than ever. The televising of the 1966 World Cup in England, criticized at first on the grounds that there was far too much of it, in fact had a colossal appeal, creating new fans and giving the English game new vitality. 800 million watched the 1970 Final.

What would the pioneers of the game, the men in knee breeches and stocking caps, have thought if they could have visualized the future? How would it have appeared to N. Lane 'Pa' Jackson, founder in the 1880s of the mighty Corinthians club, who criticized the first Football Association tour of Europe because 'professionals had been included'? How would it have seemed to the courtly Major Marindin, who played for Old Etonians and the Royal Engineers when such teams dominated the F.A. Cup, and once voluntarily left the field himself, because an opponent had been hurt and disabled?

Would the men who played the first F.A. Cup Final in 1872 in the morning, so that they could watch the Boat Race in the afternoon, have credited the scenes at Wembley Stadium each year, when 100,000 watch the Final, and another half-a-million or more would if they could? And how would the imposingly bearded Scot, William McGregor, who invented the principle of League football in the 1880s, so that professional clubs would not go short of fixtures, have viewed the present, desperate struggle for points?

The Marindins and Jacksons of their day were, after

all, alarmed enough when the new game spread beyond the public school men to the industrial working classes. They were not a bit pleased when, in the early 1880s, factory hands in Blackburn and Preston began to find 'money in their boots', when crack players arrived in Lancashire from Scotland outwardly to take jobs, but really to play football.

When supporters from Blackburn flocked into London to watch an early Cup Final at The Oval – where they were played till 1893 – a sardonic newspaper writer compared their arrival with that of a barbarian horde.

How much less would the Jacksons – and probably the McGregors – have welcomed the spread of football around the world. They saw it as a manly British game, in which hard knocks were cheerfully received and given. The South Americans and the Europeans, brilliantly though they play the game, have never quite seen it in the same way; which has been at the root of much of the trouble when British and foreign teams meet. The continentals have always been inclined to regard hard physical challenge as a form of assault and battery; a kind of violence which must be met with violence. They, after all, were not brought up like Major Marindin or Lord Kinnaird on the playing fields of Eton.

Lord Kinnaird – he, too, handsomely bearded – was a leading player in the 1870s, a Scottish international, much given to the early practice of 'hacking' – deliberately kicking an opponent – which in 1863 caused the Football Association and the Rugby Football people to go their separate ways. The story is told that on one occasion, Kinnaird's wife told a friend that she was always afraid her husband would return one day with a broken leg. 'Don't worry,' was the curt reply. 'If he does, it won't be his own.'

11

Perhaps it was to be expected that, with the gigantic development of the game, various countries would claim credit for it. The Italians have alleged that it grew from *calcio in costume*, football in costume, which was certainly played in Florence, in the Piazza delle Croce, during the sixteenth century. Indeed, it is recorded that a match was in progress at the very moment that the city was being besieged by the Emperor Charles V. Yet *calcio*, which allows players to use their hands abundantly, and has two huge goals at either end of the square, was scarcely played for several hundred years, till it was revived in the twentieth century.

Ancient paintings suggest that some form of football was played by the Chinese, who were wont to kick wicker balls, dressed in their customary robes. The most primitive football of all was probably played by savage tribes, with the heads of their defeated enemies. As for England itself, the game was certainly known as early as the fourteenth century, when various monarchs forbade it because they thought it was interfering with archery practice. For several centuries, it was a very ferocious pastime indeed – 'a bloodie and murthering practice', one chronicler called it – in which the ball was almost secondary to the violence which the players wrought on one another. Shrove Tuesday football, in the North and Midlands, saw whole towns and villages turn out to belabour each other, playing from end to end of the town.

Typically, it was the public schools, developed by Dr Arnold of Rugby and his followers, during the reign of Queen Victoria, which took the brutal, traditional game and domesticated it.

The Rules

The trouble was, so far as any unified code of rules was concerned, that every school tended to play its own kind of football. Thus, at some schools, such as Harrow, the goal ran all the way along the base line. Clearly this had much more in common with Rugby, and the scoring of tries, than with soccer, and the scoring of goals. Eton gave the game the rudiments of its vital, controversial offside rule: at Eton, it was very descriptively known as 'sneaking'. Getting behind an opposing defence and waiting for the ball to come to you was properly condemned as an unsportsmanlike act.

When the public school men got to Oxford and Cambridge, as so many of them did, it was clearly impossible for them to go on playing their separate and special codes of football. So it was that the basic laws of soccer were hammered out, particularly at Cambridge; and in 1863, at the Freemasons' Tavern, in London, the Football Association was born.

The Style of Play

In those remote days, there was no such thing as tactics. Football, indeed, till the Scots brought in the passing game, was very much a thing of individual achievement. A welter of forwards – reduced within a few years to half-a-dozen and, by the end of the century, to five – bore down on an undermanned defence. The wonder of it was that the first ever international match, between England and Scotland in Glasgow in 1872, should have ended in a goalless draw.

When a forward got the ball, his one purpose was to dribble past as many defenders as possible, and to try to score. This explained the success of many players from Charterhouse School, which had moved from London to Godalming, Surrey, in 1872, and practised something known as Run About. This involved as many boys as wished to take part – and a football. The object, quite simply, was to keep the ball in your possession for as long as you possibly could. Charterhouse produced, in the strapping W. N. Cobbold, a player who came to be known as The Prince of Dribblers. But the development in Scotland of the Passing Game put an end to Cobbold and his spectacular breed.

It seems strange that passing had in any sense to be 'invented', so logical does it seem to kick the ball, when you can make no further progress, to a colleague who is better placed and unmarked. But perhaps it is a still more human attribute to keep something – whether it be a secret, a bag of sweets or a football – to yourself for as long as you possibly can.

Professionalism grew up in the 1880s for two reasons; first, because there was greater and greater rivalry between the newly formed Lancashire clubs – Preston North End, Blackburn Olympic, Blackburn Rovers – second, because the new kind of player, often brought down from Scotland, was not a wealthy amateur of the kind of Kinnaird, but a relatively poor man who could afford to take off time from work only if someone made up the money he would lose.

The Corinthians

I suppose you could say that the two key figures of the 1880s in football were, at one pole, 'Pa' Jackson, and at the other, Major Sudell. We already know about Jackson, the founder of the great Corinthians. His object was to create a solid foundation for the England team, which at that time was losing most of its matches. This he did with such success that, before long, complete England teams were made up of Corinthian players. Amateurs, you will see, were still very much more than holding their own with the paid players, and they would continue to do so, right up to the start of the First World War, in 1914. Even in the early 1920s, several amateur players from the Corinthians, the Casuals and elsewhere, played for the full English international team, and one of them, A. G. Bower, a full-back from Charterhouse, actually captained the side.

'Pa' Jackson, as we have seen, snobbishly abominated professionals and professionalism. He was, however, a superb organizer, a great founder of clubs of every kind, and his Corinthian teams were a fine blend of the robust and the scientific. Though they produced, in yet another Old Carthusian, G. O. Smith, 'a very gentle, parfait knight', one of the most technically gifted and elegantly dangerous centre-forwards the game has known, there was always plenty of beef and brawn in the side. The other Carthusians, the full-backs A. M. and P. M. Walters, known, inevitably, as 'Morning' and 'Afternoon', provided that.

G. O. Smith has told the story of how, after dropping out of football for a time, they returned to play in a Cup-tie at the old Crystal Palace ground, dear to the Corinthians, against Sheffield Wednesday. A Wednesday forward gave P. M. Walters what Smith described as 'a nasty hack on the calf', and Walters, with a bellow of rage, set off in warm pursuit. The forward fled – beyond the touchline – but Walters, catching him at last, laid him low with a hefty shoulder charge, then peacefully trotted back to resume the game. The rest of the players were helplessly overcome with laughter.

Shoulder charging played a very important part in the methods of the old Corinthians. One story which they used to tell, with a manly chortle, concerned a match against some Northern team who offended them with their lack of sportsmanship. The hefty Corinthians thereafter went ponderously downfield, shoulder charging any man who tried to take the ball, till at last they reached the goal, and scored.

G. O. Smith has said that the old Corinthians never trained, which makes one wonder not only how good *they* were, but how good were the old-time professionals against whom they played with such success.

Preston, with whom Major Sudell became, perhaps, the first manager of a professional club, were certainly a mighty team. Within a relatively short time, they had surpassed Blackburn Rovers – who won the F.A. Cup three times in a row between 1884 and 1886 – and were consistently challenged only by a new club from Birmingham, Aston Villa. The Corinthians, unfortunately, would not enter for the F.A. Cup – run then, as now, as a knock-out competition, building to a Final between the last surviving clubs – otherwise the dominance of these professional clubs might have been broken.

The Football League

Needless to say, the Corinthians took no part in the Football League, when it was founded in 1888. William McGregor's idea was simple but marvellously practical. Until the League began, with a single division of a dozen clubs, professional clubs could play only F.A. Cup-ties – in which they might be quickly knocked out of the Cup – and friendly matches. This meant that, while they were obliged to pay their players every week, they could not guarantee a weekly game to bring them spectators. League football, with each of the clubs which took part playing the others at home and away, gaining two points for a win and one for a draw, provided that guarantee. Preston won the first and the second League Championships, and came to be known as 'The Invincibles'. In one Cup-tie, they defeated a team called Hyde 26–0. They won their first League title without losing a match, and carried off the Cup into the bargain without giving away a goal. This feat was not equalled till 1903, by Bury; and you can gauge the strength of the Corinthians of those days by the fact that they defeated Bury's Cup Final team, which had not conceded a goal, by 9–3!

John Goodall

One of the stars of that Preston team was a slender, delicate-looking inside-forward called John Goodall. An English international of Scottish descent, he was an early illustration of one of soccer's lasting attractions: that physique does not make the footballer. Goodall looked as if a strong gust of wind might cause him serious difficulty, but it did not stop him being a formidably skilful and effective player. Behind him played the huge, protective figure of his big brother Archie, a muscular centre-half. If an opponent ill-treated John, then Archie would growl, 'Getting rough, son? I'll *lean* against you in a moment!'

Scottish Football

Goodall, and Preston, exemplified the Scottish school of football, which set the pattern not only for Britain, but for the world. Classic Scottish football was played along the ground, rhythmically and perhaps a little slowly, with an emphasis on highly skilled ball control, shrewd positional play, and both moving and passing into the

17

open space. Thanks to famous English coaches such as Jimmy Hogan, of whom we shall be hearing more, these methods were brought first to Europe, then to South America, where they took root and survived till long after they had been abandoned in England: and even, alas, in Scotland.

The new English professional clubs drew heavily from the first on Scottish talent, while the Scots, despite their huge inferiority in numbers, for many years to come had the better of matches against England. Meanwhile, the game was quickly developing. Soon tapes gave way in the goals to crossbars, while in 1891, at the suggestion of the Irish Association, the penalty kick was introduced. The goalkeeper, already the only man on the field to be allowed to use his hands, except for the throw-in, was gradually restricted to the penalty area; for some years, he had been actually and happily allowed to bounce the ball downfield to his heart's content.

By the last years of the nineteenth century, soccer had already won the hearts of the industrial masses, who swarmed to important matches in their thousands; though the professional game was a good deal slower to develop in the South. When the Cup Final changed its home from The Oval, more traditionally associated with cricket, to the Crystal Palace, crowds rose above 100,000.

Bill Foulke

There were some unusual, not to say eccentric, figures among the leading players of the day. Word came out of Derbyshire of a giant goalkeeper called Bill Foulke who, in a charity match, had punched John Goodall instead of the ball, and knocked out a couple of his teeth. The colossal Foulke, whose playing weight would eventually reach twenty-three stone, signed for Sheffield

18

United, played for England, and became one of the great goalkeepers of his day.

Despite his massive girth, there was nothing placid about him. He was, indeed, a very emotional man who, if he felt his defence had let him down, was quite capable of standing still and making no effort to prevent a goal. If forwards annoyed him by trying to charge or bustle him, he might lift them up with one great arm and throw them into the back of his net.

One centre-forward called Harry Hampton, of Aston Villa, was particularly given to tormenting goalkeepers. In a match against Sheffield United, he somehow managed to avoid hitting Foulke – no small feat in itself – and to land upside down, tangled helplessly in the goal netting. Foulke simply allowed him to hang there, paying no heed to his pleas.

'Tha got oop there,' said Foulke, cuttingly, 'tha can get thysen down.'

He could, as you may imagine, be a terrifying fellow when he lost his temper. This happened on the occasion of a Cup Final at the Crystal Palace, when Foulke believed that one of the goals scored against him, and Sheffield United, had been offside. After the match, he went, stark naked, looking for the referee. Luckily, as the vast figure padded down the dressing-room corridor, one of the linesmen managed to shout a warning to the referee to lock his door; which he did just in time. Foulke was eventually pacified by various officials, among them the Secretary of the Football Association.

In 1905, when the Chelsea club was formed, Foulke was bought by them as their first goalkeeper; a spectacular attraction for south-west London. Once, at an away match in the North, a group of rival supporters met Chelsea's train, carrying a placard inscribed, COME AND SEE CHELSEA'S 24-STONE GOALKEEPER.

'Twenty-four stun!' rumbled Foulke. 'I'll give 'em twenty-four stun!' He shuffled his feet, and the men ran away.

Steve Bloomer

Foulke himself, however, was known to run away on at least one occasion; when playing against another hero of the period, Steve Bloomer, the most formidable goal-scorer of his day, and perhaps – till Pelé – of any day. Bloomer was another of those slender, pale-looking creatures who was, in fact, capable of great feats of power. He had an unusually strong shot in his right foot, with which he scored literally hundreds of goals for Derby County, Middlesbrough and England, thanks partly to the great speed with which he could kick the ball. There was not much back lift to his shot, as they would say in cricket, and he tended to hit the ball well up on the instep, quite near to the toe.

It was said that the sight of Foulke's enormous stomach in goal was a temptation Bloomer could never resist, and in one game he twice knocked the giant out with tremendous shots to the belly. On the third occasion, the ball sailed straight into the goal. 'Foulke,' as one observer recalled it, 'had incontinently fled.'

The game continued to be very hard and robust, up to the Great War. Charlie Buchan, a Londoner of Scots parentage who became one of the best inside-forwards of his day, told the story of an early First Division game for Sunderland against Notts County. He was, at the time, a long, thin figure – though war service would fill him out and strengthen him – and he was opposed by a squat, tough little full-back called Montgomery. Early in the game, he received the ball, tapped it past Montgomery on the inside, and raced past him down the touchline, on the outside. 'Don't do that again, son,' said Montgomery. But Buchan, full of the joys of youth and success, did do it again; to find himself charged bodily almost into the surrounding wall. 'They were tough,' he wrote, 'in those days.'

2. The World Takes To It

International Football

Believe it or not, the world's governing body of football, FIFA – otherwise the International Federation of Association Football – was founded as early as 1904. Its inspiration was French; as so much else in football was to be, including the World Cup and the European Cup. The French pioneers of FIFA persisted despite a cool lack of encouragement across the Channel. When one of their leaders came to London to see Lord Kinnaird, President by now of the F.A., he went home in despair to complain, 'It was like beating the air'. Quite simply, the British did not want anybody else to help them run football. Though one or two rare and far-sighted critics such as the tiny James Catton, editor of the old *Athletic News*, warned against such complacency – 'write me down senile and silly, but the truth will prevail and this is the truth' – the general attitude was insular in the extreme. Foreign football was in its infancy: 'I have seen it grow,' Jimmy Hogan would say, in years to come, 'from a weakling into a strong man.' These were the days of enthusiasm – and little more – but how quickly the picture would change.

The first, historic Football Association tour of Germany was made in 1899. Relations between Britain and Germany were bad at the time, but the Schricker brothers, who did so much for the establishment of football in Germany, defied political pressure, borrowed money from their mother, and saw that the tour went on.

The English party included famous amateur and professional players, among them the celebrated Billy Bassett, outside-right of West Bromwich Albion and England – whose celebrity had gone before him. So much so, indeed, that in one match a German defender called Westermarck, a large young man with the caste mark of a duelling scar down one cheek, was detailed to follow Bassett wherever he went; and did so. To such an extent, indeed, that when Bassett whimsically strolled off the field, round the German goalposts, and back on to the field again, Westermarck, with German literal-mindedness, followed his every step.

This mixed amateur and professional tour of Germany was a great success, off as well as on the field. 'Strange to relate,' wrote the *Athletic News*, with a caustic dig at 'Pa' Jackson, 'the professionals managed to behave themselves.'

In 1901, the Germans returned the visit, playing two international matches, one at Tottenham against an England team made up of amateurs, which beat them 12–0, the other against a team of professionals in Manchester – who beat them 10–0, despite the wish expressed by the *Manchester Guardian* that courtesy and a sense of hospitality would move the professionals to let the Germans off more lightly than had the amateurs.

All over the world, football was growing apace. In Austria, English gardeners working on Baron Rothschild's estates brought the game to Vienna, where the first club was known as The Cricketers. A group of British expatriates in Genoa formed the Genoa Football and Cricket Club, still known in Italy as *il vecchio Genoa*, old Genoa. For some years, they refused to allow Italians to join! In Argentina, frequently visited by leading professional teams before the Great War, Englishmen formed the nucleus of the international side; though the game did not really catch alight till the massive emigration from Italy, in those years. In Brazil, the driving enthusiasm of an English expatriate working in the railways led to the founding of the earliest clubs. In Denmark, British schoolboys brought their game with them. In Russia, the two Lancastrian Charnock brothers taught football to their mill workers, not far from Moscow, using strap-piercing machines to attach studs to ordinary boots.

When the Olympic Games were held in London for the first time, in 1908, there was a football tournament, of a miniature kind. Trouble in the creaking Austro-Hungarian Empire alas prevented the Hungarians – who were already playing full internationals against the England team – from coming; but the powerful Danes came, the Dutch and Swedes came, while the French sent two teams.

The Danes

The Danes were already astonishingly good. Tall and well made, they played a straightforward, English type of football, thrashed both French teams in a welter of goals, and played a splendid Final against a strong United Kingdom team, consisting of leading amateurs.

25

One of them, Vivian Woodward, was among the out-standing inside-forwards of his day, playing many fine games for the full England team, not to mention Spurs and Chelsea.

In the event, England won by only 2–0, and were a little lucky to do so; poor finishing let the Danes down, as it would continue to let foreign teams down, till Hungary came to Wembley in 1953 to smash England's unbeaten record. In 1912, when the Olympic Games were played in Stockholm, and a far larger field entered the soccer tournament, the Danes again gave the United Kingdom a very close run in the Final, losing 4–2 after playing most of the game with ten men. One of their players, Nils Middelboe, the left-half, would become a distinguished captain of Chelsea after the war.

So high were his amateur principles that when New-castle United persuaded him to join them, and to take a job in the Danish Consulate in Newcastle, he turned them down on discovering that Newcastle had secretly agreed to pay part of his wages at the Consulate.

Jimmy Hogan

Not until 1953 would a foreign team – the Hungarians – come to England and win a full international. On that November day, a little, white-haired Englishman sat in the Royal Box at Wembley, watching with a mixture of pride and intense disappointment; the guest, not of the Football Association, but of the Hungarians. That man was Jimmy Hogan.

He was born in the little Lancashire town of Nelson, and became an inside-right of modest abilities; though Ireland nearly chose him once for an international match, in the mistaken belief that he was an Irishman. In later years, he would say that he really learned about the game when he was playing for Fulham, and that the people whom he learned from were the Scottish professionals who were playing for Fulham at the time.

He did some coaching in Holland. Then, in 1912, the equally remarkable Hugo Meisl brought him to Vienna to coach the Austrians.

Meisl was really the father of Austrian football. Born into a wealthy Jewish family in Vienna, it was perhaps his admiration for all things English which first caused him to play football for the Cricketers club. He was a fragile but, apparently, quite gifted inside-forward. So passionate was his interest in the game that his father, who felt it was interfering with his business career, packed him off to the Italian port of Trieste, which was then in the Austrian Empire. But Hugo was not a whit put out; he simply kept in regular correspondence with Johann Leute, one of the best Austrian footballers of the period. So when he returned to Vienna to become a leading figure in the Austrian Football Federation, he was well informed on all that had gone on.

When Hogan got to Vienna, his first day's coaching was a disaster. As he told Hugo Meisl afterwards, in despair, he had shown the Viennese players what he always showed his pupils; but somehow, he had not put it across to them. Meisl thought he knew what was wrong, had a long talk with Hogan – and from that moment, as they say, the penny dropped. Hogan understood his Austrian pupils, his pupils understood him, and the basis for a long and famous association had been built.

Hogan taught the Austrians Scottish football; and they loved it. They were mostly well educated young men from the university, and 'scientific' football appealed to them. They liked the idea of making steady, rhythmic progress by passing the ball along the ground, with such

27

inevitability that a goal, at last, just had to be scored. Hogan told the story of how, strolling through the streets of Vienna one evening, he came across a group of young Austrians playing football, watched by a man who kept shouting at them, 'Don't kick it, push it; don't kick it, push it!' This led to the attractive, flowing Vienna School of football, the trouble with which was that, though it pleased the eye, it did not always bring results. To score goals, you sometimes have to forsake attractive football for direct methods.

However, Viennese football made very rapid progress under Hogan and Meisl, and soon they were capable of beating a strong Tottenham Hotspur side. One of the most popular early visits was made by Southampton, who were very adventurous tourists. They had a famous English international goalkeeper called Jack Robinson, and before one of the matches in Austria the Austrians insisted that he give a goalkeeping exhibition. The rest of the Southampton players obligingly shot straight at him, but the Viennese crowd loved it, and for years afterwards referred to a particularly fine save as a 'Robinsonade'.

When the Great War broke out, Hogan was interned by the Austrians, but they soon released him, and he was able to coach not only there but in Hungary, where his methods were just as eagerly accepted. The Hungarians had already come a long way from the legendary day when a visiting English goalkeeper had so little to do that he allegedly sat on the crossbar, smoking his pipe. They, like the Austrians, were naturally gifted ball-players, and if the sturdy Danes so far led the field in European football, it would not be long before the Hungarians overtook them.

Meanwhile, during these early years of Continental football, a poor Italian student called Vittorio Pozzo was living in England, making a living by teaching languages all over the Midlands; and spending his Saturdays watching the fine Manchester United team of the era.

Pozzo came from the northern province of Piedmont, near Turin; he was always happiest among the mountains. He came to London to learn English, found 'too many Italians looking for one another and spending evenings with each other', so moved farther North, to be among the English. He liked the life so much that he refused his family's orders to come home. When they cut off his allowance, he began teaching languages to make up for it. He admired tremendously the Manchester United centre-half, Charlie Roberts, one of the leading players of his day; an all-round, attacking player, as centre-halves then were.

One afternoon, having seen a match, he shyly waited outside the ground for the great Roberts to appear. When he did, he approached him, introduced himself, and asked whether he might talk to him about football. Roberts agreed. It was the first of many conversations, which formed the basis for the tactics Pozzo would use to win the World Cups of 1934 and 1938. He always wanted, in his Italian teams of the era, an attacking centre-half cast in the mould of Roberts, who would send long passes to the wings. So at a time when Britain had given up the attacking centre-half for the third-back 'stopper', Italy carried on successfully with the 'old-fashioned' roamer. But more of all that in its place.

It was Pozzo who, at the last moment, took an Italian team to the Stockholm Olympics of 1912. His family had lured him home, inviting him to his sister's wedding, and sending him a return ticket. When he got back to Italy, they insisted that he stay. In 1953, when I visited him in Turin, he still had the unused half of that return ticket.

Curiously enough, Steve Bloomer, like Hogan, was also trapped in Europe when the war broke out – in Germany, itself – and he too was allowed to stay and coach, throughout the war. So British coaches took the game to the corners of the earth; but they found they were prophets without honour in their own country. Even Hogan would learn, to his painful surprise, that the British did not believe in coaching. They were far too thoroughly convinced that they were born footballers, while foreign players had to be made.

3. The Game Changes

The Offside Law

Round about 1924, football in Britain began to be impossible. Professional football, that is to say, as played by certain professional defenders. The reason that it became impossible is that these defenders were making use of the offside law to make life miserable for forwards.

At that time, the offside law ruled that, to be onside, a player had to have *three* men between himself and the opposing goal-line, *at the time the ball was last played.* You can simplify this by saying that he needed two men between himself and the opposing goalkeeper. Morley and Montgomery, the two Notts County full-backs, had already made use of this rule by moving cunningly up-field, to put the enemy forwards in an offside position; but this was nothing to the methods of the Newcastle United backs, McCracken and Hudspeth.

Bill McCracken, a cheerful Irishman, was among the finest defenders of his day, and had been an outstanding member of the brilliant pre-war Newcastle United team which had excelled in Cup and League. McCracken was a strong, stylish player who could have held his own perfectly well, without the aid of the notorious offside trap. Having known him in later years, I suspect that he got a certain wicked amusement out of it all.

What he and Hudspeth did was very simple, but horridly effective. They simply waited till an attack developed, whereupon one or other would glide upfield, the linesman's flag would go up, the referee's whistle would blow – and Newcastle would have yet another free kick for offside. The story is told that a dejected visiting team arrived one day at Newcastle station, a guard's whistle blew, and one of their players remarked, 'Blimey, offside already'.

Something had to happen, if the game was not going to become a dreary stalemate, confined to midfield, endlessly punctuated by the referee's whistle. The British football associations, who controlled – as they still do, by a majority of four to two – the rule-making International Board, put their heads together. They held a trial match in which offside was limited to certain areas of the field, decided against that, and cut down the number of men required between a forward and the goal-line from three to two. It was a historic decision, and people are still arguing about whether or not it was a correct one. Some believe that it was too hasty; that it would have been more sensible to keep the old, three-man rule, and concentrate on specifying 'offside' areas on the pitch.

Dixie Dean

At all events, the balance for a while was tipped sharply in favour of the forwards. Although Arsenal were very quick to develop the third-back game with its 'policeman' centre-half, the attackers held the whip hand for some years. In the season 1927–8, Bill 'Dixie' Dean, Everton's centre-forward, a renowned header of a ball, scored the amazing total of sixty First Division goals; a record which will surely stand to the end of time; or at least of football.

Tall, dark haired and very powerful, Dean's skill and strength with his head gave birth to the fable of how he once ran across Elisha Scott, the famous Irish international goalkeeper of Everton's local rivals, Liverpool, on a station platform. Dean nodded; and Scott, with a pure reflex action, flung himself full length on the station platform.

Tactics

Certainly some kind of change had to be made in the rules. What is interesting is that nobody had ever tried to exploit them in this way before. The rule, after all, had existed, ready to be used by cunning defenders, from the beginning of football. What had happened, it seems to me, was a change of heart; the kind of thing, no doubt, that the 'Pa' Jacksons and Major Marindins of this world had feared, as a product of the growth of professionalism. Results were becoming too important. The game was no longer the thing; how could it be when men had their livings at stake?

So the tactical formation would change. Before the alteration in the offside law, just in time for season 1925–6, a team would line up with this disposition:

33

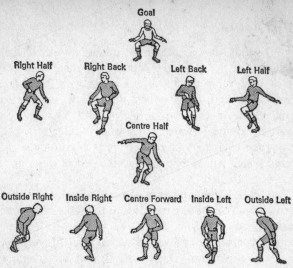

Goal

Right Half   Right Back   Left Back   Left Half

Centre Half

Outside Right Inside Right Centre Forward Inside Left Outside Left

You will see that the wing-half-backs played out on
the flanks, marking the wingers. But their job did not
end there, for they were also expected to be attackers,
taking the ball upfield after intercepting it or winning a
tackle, and feeding their own forwards. No wonder wing-
half was considered just about the most tiring and
demanding position on the field. Funnily enough, in
today's football, the full-back has, so to speak, come full
circle. He is playing very much as the wing-halves used
to play, before the game changed. We hear a great deal
about 'overlapping' full-backs; meaning full-backs who
attack by running on down the touchline, past their own
winger; or where their winger would be if they played
with one: some teams use only one, some none at all.
Full-backs such as Tony Dunne of Manchester United,
Terry Cooper of Leeds United and Tommy Gemmell of
Celtic, delight in racing upfield with the ball; just as
wing-half-backs used to do. But when the game changed,
and the full-backs were brought out of the middle to

mark the wingers, they became [...] simple for the next forty years or so. [...]ers pure and say that they stayed defenders; for [...]er, one might were when they played beefily in the m[...] what they

The old attacking or 'roving' centre-ha[...] wing-halves for energy and activity. Often a[...]alled his ward would drop back, or 'deep' as we say, t[...] side-for-[...]p him.

The wingers, in the manner of the renow[...] Billy Meredith, a Welsh international who played till [...] was nearly fifty, generally kept well out on the flank, ra[...]for the corner flag, and dropped their high centres into [...]e goalmouth.

Arsenal

The changed offside rule threw all this into the melting pot; and it was Arsenal, till then a mediocre London club who only twelve years earlier had moved from south-east London to Highbury, in north London, who led the way. They had just appointed as manager Herbert Chapman, who, in the previous two seasons, had led Huddersfield Town to the League Championship. Chapman, in turn, brought the long-legged Charlie Buchan from Sunderland. Buchan, a veteran by now, had once been an amateur on the books of Arsenal, in their Woolwich days, but had left the club after an argument over eleven shillings' worth of expenses. Now, to get him back, Arsenal had to pay £2,500 down – and to promise £100 for every goal he scored that season. It was typical of the adventurous kind of deal Herbert Chapman would do. Buchan was to prove a wonderful capture; his captaincy, his skilful play and his marksmanship had much to do with Arsenal's swift rise. So did the tactical plan which he now – after Arsenal had lost their first match heavily at Newcastle – suggested to Chapman.

He wanted the attacking centre-half pulled back into

the defence in midfield, one inside-forward would play behind the rest of the forward-line, while the wing-half would now move into the middle of the field, marking the opposing inside-forwards. Meanwhile, the full-backs would move out on to the flanks, to mark the wingers. Buchan expected himself to be given the job of the deep-lying inside-forward, but in the event Chapman brought in a third-team player called Andy Neil to fill the role, in a mid-week match at West Ham. Arsenal won comfortably; and the third-back game had for better or for worse been born.

This is how the formation would now look:

Goal

Right Back   Centre Half   Left Back

Right Half   Left Half

Inside Right   Inside Left

Outside Right   Centre Forward   Outside Left

You will see that the other inside-forward, too, had been pulled out of the forward-line to become a fetcher-and-carrier. This led to a system known as the W formation; if you draw a line linking up the five forwards, you will see why. The wingers and centre-forward now carried the burden of scoring goals, though at least one of the inside-forwards was likely to help them from time to time. The centre-forward, meanwhile, was going to have a much harder life than in the past, for the third back, the stopper centre-half, would have the almost exclusive job of marking him. Thus the centre-half, once the most creative and adventurous player in any football team, would now become the most negative and destructive. Centre-halves and centre-forwards would cancel each other out to such an extent that it was said of them that they might often just as well sit and play cards in the dressing-room.

For Arsenal, the new tactics were wonderfully effective. Never previously winners of Cup or League, they embarked on an astonishing period of success, which lasted right up to the outbreak of the Second World War in September, 1939.

Herbert Chapman

For this Herbert Chapman, though he died early in 1934, took much if not most of the credit. Certainly he was one of the outstanding football managers the game has ever known, deeply respected and admired not only by his own players and in England at large, but by men such as Pozzo and Meisl, though they had had much better formal educations than he. Chapman was a Yorkshireman, a professional footballer in his day, of no great note. He had been a reserve with Tottenham Hotspur, conspicuous largely for the strange yellow colour of his football boots.

He later became player-manager of Northampton Town, who were not yet then in the Football League – which consisted till after the Great War of two divisions – and then manager of Leeds City. But the Leeds club, forerunner of Leeds United, was accused of making illegal payments to players, and was disbanded by the Football Association and the League. Chapman was banned from football; a harsh punishment which was soon, happily, lifted. It was typical of him, meanwhile, that when he was asked for the club's account books, giving details of the payments they were supposed to have made, he replied briefly and bluntly, 'I've burned them'. The interests of his players always came first.

I have spoken of his success with Huddersfield Town, where he left enough impetus for the club to win the Championship for a third successive season – a record later equalled by Arsenal – after he had left them. When he came to Arsenal, it was to a club with no past to speak of. But his tactical grasp and his remarkable ability to choose and inspire the right men soon worked wonders.

Tom Whittaker

One of the first and most important things Chapman did at Arsenal was to appoint a new club trainer: Tom Whittaker. Whittaker, a powerfully made North-Easterner, had been left-half in the Arsenal First Division team; a strong, brave rather than a gifted player. That summer – 1925 – he was a member of the Football Association party, severely broke a leg, and came home thoroughly anxious, knowing his career was over.

Chapman surprised and delighted him by making him trainer. In some remarkable way, he had guessed at Whittaker's extraordinary powers of healing; powers which would play a vital role in Arsenal's success. It has been said that where, in any other club, an injured player might be out of the game for weeks, Whittaker would have him back on the field in a matter of days. This, moreover, was in the days when a trainer had few magical machines to assist him; no ultra-sonic waves, no deep diathermy heat. Whittaker used his strong hands, and his unusual powers of diagnosis – of seeing, or brilliantly guessing, what was wrong and what had to be done.

Arsenal reached their first Cup Final in 1927, and lost it in a heartbreaking way. Finals, by now, were played at Wembley Stadium, which had grown up on the site of the Wembley Exhibition of the early 1920s. In 1923, when the first Cup Final was played at Wembley, more than 200,000 people crowded into the stadium, a policeman on a white horse helped to keep the throng in order, and the match was played with the spectators almost up to the touchline. Bolton beat West Ham United 2–0, and the West Ham captain, Jack Tresadern, always said that the best pass he had all afternoon came from a spectator. Another West Ham player, more seriously, disappeared into the crowd, chasing a ball, and could not get back before Bolton scored a goal.

But to return to 1927: Arsenal lost the Cup to Cardiff City, the only time the trophy has ever gone out of England, to one of the strangest goals seen at Wembley. Ferguson, Cardiff's Scottish centre-forward, shot, without any great force or danger. Danny Lewis, Arsenal's talented Welsh international goalkeeper, went down for the ball; the easiest and most straightforward of saves – or so it appeared. But suddenly the ball seemed to be wriggling in his arms as though it were alive. Desperately he clutched at it, but it spun out of his grasp, away and over the line, to give Cardiff City a strange victory.

Three years later, with a much changed team – the team, more or less, with which they would dominate English football in the 1930s – they were at Wembley again; and this time they won. Suitably enough, their opponents, and victims, had been the other team which Chapman built: Huddersfield Town. 2–0 was the score: but two years later, Arsenal would not be so fortunate.

Newcastle United beat them, thanks largely to another very strange goal. Arsenal were leading 1–0 when Richardson, the Newcastle inside-right, chased a long pass to the right-hand goal-line. The ball seemed quite clearly to go out of play. So the whole Arsenal defence thought, for they stopped; but Richardson didn't. He chased the ball, reached it, centred, and Allen, the centre-forward, headed into the net. The referee, despite Arsenal's dismayed protests, gave a goal, Newcastle got the upper hand, and Allen scored again to give them the Cup, 2–1.

The Arsenal's tactics were criticized by many at the time, and have been criticized by many later; not least because they had such a tremendous influence on British football at every level. Indeed, the third-back game and the W formation virtually ruled European football till Brazil brought in 4–2–4 in 1958. It was essentially defensive. Herbert Chapman used to tell his teams that, in a League match, they went out on to the field with one point; if they did not give away a goal, they came off with at least one point. Arsenal, though they had many brilliant players, such as Eddie Hapgood, at left-back, Alex James, in midfield, and David Jack, who once swerved past five Aston Villa defenders to score an extraordinary goal, were chiefly a defensive team. Just as some boxers are counter-punchers, never leading themselves, but waiting for their opponents to throw a punch and leave themselves open, so Arsenal were the first to practise what is so common in football today: the counter-attack. Cliff Bastin, their gifted outside-left, who was a star at seventeen and had won every honour in the game at nineteen, once said that when Arsenal had too much of the play they became worried.

Arsenal's critics insisted that with so many fine players, they could have succeeded with whatever tactics they cared to use; which may or may not be true. As it was, in those fourteen years which followed Chapman's arrival and preceded the outbreak of war, they won the League Championship five times and the Cup twice, were runners-up twice in the Cup Final, and came second in the League (as well as losing the Final) in season 1931–2.

Alex James

Alex James, a tough little Scot from Bellshill, who came to Arsenal in 1929 from Preston North End, was unquestionably the key player in the team. Small but very strong, his beautifully judged and powerfully struck passes from midfield, some through the middle to a charging, challenging centre-forward, some 'inside' the full-back to Bastin, on the left wing, some across field to the racing Joe Hulme, were of priceless effect.

With Preston, he had not played that kind of game at all, but Chapman, characteristically, saw in him the potential to grow into a much more mature and versatile player than he was, and bought him for £9,000. It took a few months for the change to be made, and even when James had settled down, there were still occasional rows and ructions.

Everyone sooner or later followed Arsenal; even the Scots. Alas, they were sadly eager to throw over their splendid, slower, traditional football, even though they had kept comfortably ahead of the England team in international matches, even since the Great War. Rangers and Celtic, the two great Glasgow clubs, one with its Protestant, the other with its Catholic associations, did not resist the 'new', machine-like football for long. By 1933, when Scotland and Austria drew at Hampden Park, the immense shrine of Scottish football owned by the Queens Park amateur club, Hugo Meisl was describing the Scots game as one based on speed and force. What changes had taken place!

Yet for many years to come, the Scottish game was still slower and more thoughtful than the English, and it was generally considered that a Scots player who crossed the border into English football required time to adjust to the quicker pace. Nevertheless, it is worth noticing that Rangers had the better of their long series of friendly matches against Arsenal, through the 1930s.

Coaches like Jimmy Hogan lamented the new brand of football, in which science – at least in terms of individual skill – had been sacrificed to speed. Tactics, however, were a good deal more scientific, even if, in this day and age, they may seem rather crude by comparison with the carefully laid plans of the 1960s and 70s.

The third-back game was always vulnerable to Alex James's swinging crossfield pass, because its defences were based on zonal covering. Defenders, that is to say, normally marked a given area of space, rather than a man, the full-backs and the centre-half pivoting to face, in a diagonal line, whichever wing danger might be coming from. If the backs played too closely to the opposing wingers, they were said, in football parlance, to be too 'square', too much in a line, thus leaving gaps in the middle. But if a full-back moved away from his wing to give cover to his centre-half – who was watching the other flank, from which danger came – he obviously had to leave his winger uncovered. 4–2–4, which put a wing-half-back beside the centre-half, would end this, but it lay a very long way in the future. Meanwhile, Italy, Austria and the South American countries stayed faithful to the attacking centre-half. Italy did not abandon him till early in the Second World War, while Austria retained him till the middle 1950s.

International Matches

In 1932, when Hugo Meisl and Jimmy Hogan brought Austria to London for a famous match against England – which they lost but deserved to win – Hogan took all his players to watch Chelsea play Everton, at Stamford Bridge. (The international match took place there, four days later.)

Two of the game's finest centre-forwards, in their different ways, were playing: the burly Dixie Dean for Everton, the tiny, explosive Hughie Gallacher, for Chelsea. Each side, Hogan complained, simply banged the ball high and hopefully down the middle for the centre-forward: in almost every case, the centre-half rose and headed it away again.

Four years earlier, in what was perhaps the final flourish of classical Scottish football, Gallacher had figured with James, his boyhood friend from Bellshill, in a marvellous Scottish forward-line which destroyed England's defence at Wembley. Every man but Alec Jackson, the outside-right, who scored three goals, was tiny; but they ran the English side ragged on the thick Wembley turf, winning 5–1. The outside-left, another marvellous ball-player, and very fast, withal, was Alan Morton of Rangers. In boyhood, he had practised his skill by endlessly trying to kick a tennis ball through a narrow hole in the coal-shed door.

The following year – in May, 1929, to be precise – England lost to a foreign team for the first time. They were beaten 4–3 in Madrid, by a Spanish side which included an illustrious goalkeeper in Ricardo Zamora. It was appallingly hot; so hot that the Spanish trainer kept running on to the field to dash water into the faces of his players, and the English team was tired at the end of its long tour. But the fact remains that it was a strong team, which was expected to win without much difficulty.

In 1931, Spain came to London, the crowd stormed the gates of the Arsenal Stadium, Zamora had one of his very, very few poor matches, gave away two early, easy goals – and England won 7–1 in the mud. 'If Zamora earns £50 a week,' wrote an English critic, 'then Hibbs [England's goalkeeper] deserves a benefit once a fortnight.' It should be mentioned that English footballers of that time – and right up to the Second World War – earned a princely £8 a week. The League clubs had taken ruthless advantage of unemployment in the 1920s to push the wage down from £9 a week; and there they relentlessly kept it.

In 1930, Austria's so-called *Wunderteam* (wonder team), playing what was once traditional Scottish football, held England to a 0–0 draw in Vienna. The following year, again in Vienna, it thrashed a Scottish team which unwisely went abroad without Rangers or Celtic players, 5–0. Then, in 1932, came that exciting, see-sawing match at Chelsea, which England won 4–3. Thanks to these victories at home, England were able to ignore the writing on the wall, provided by defeats abroad which took place in the close season.

'Wait till we get them in our English mud!' became the cry. But a time would come when foreign footballers lost their fear of London, learned how to shoot, and overcame even the English mud.

4. The World Cup Begins

Jules Rimet

Though no British team competed in it till 1950, the World Cup actually began as early as 1930. Foreign countries were always anxious to have British leadership, particularly the inventive French, but when it was not forthcoming, they were ready enough to go ahead on their own.

The World Cup was the idea of Jules Rimet, a French football administrator after whom, in fact, the trophy was named. During the Second World War, he kept the little gold cup under his bed, for fear that the German occupying forces would steal it; and melt it down. The idea wasn't particularly new, even as long ago as 1930. What brought it to birth was, above all, the rise of professionalism, which was making a farce out of the

47

only existing international football tournament, the Olympic Games.

Olympic Games

These were resumed in 1920, and it quickly became clear that since they had last taken place, in 1912, a great deal had changed. In the first place, European football had grown much stronger. In the second, the Danes no longer led the Continent. Britain sent a strong team, which was promptly despatched by little Norway. The Final was eventually contested by Belgium, the hosts – the games were played in Antwerp – and Czechoslovakia.

The match, unfortunately, ended in a way which was all too accurately to foreshadow the course of international football. The English referee, a bearded veteran called Mr John Lewis, who had been kicked by a spectator twelve years earlier while refereeing a Bohemia v. England match in Prague, found it hard to control matters. Eventually, a Czech brutally fouled a Belgian, Lewis sent him off the field – and the other Czech players immediately followed him. There was nothing to do but to award the prize to Belgium. Second place went to Spain, for whom the dashing Zamora was playing in his first major tournament. They greatly surprised everybody with their fire and skill.

Uruguay

But in 1924, when the Olympic Games were held in Paris, Europe found it had a new force to contend with: South America. Britain did not send a team; they were already uneasy about sham amateurism in the Games, the reason for their withdrawal, four years later, from FIFA itself. But the Uruguayans went, saw and conquered. Their splendid team, combining great skill on the ball with direct, thrustful attack, had splendid forwards in Pedro Petrone and Scarone.

In the Final, Uruguay comfortably beat a useful Swiss team 3–0. But the whole tournament fairly reeked of professionalism: still more so at Amsterdam, in 1928, when Uruguay retained their title, beating Argentina 2–1 in the Final, after a 1–1 draw.

The Agentinians brought with them some splendid players, particularly a fast, dangerous outside-left called Raimondo Orsi, and a tough, ruthless centre-half called Luisito Monti. Both of them later joined the Juventus club of Turin, and played for Italy in the World Cup of 1934. Under Italian law, foreigners of Italian descent automatically had Italian nationality, and Vittorio Pozzo was quick to put such stars in his Italian team. To critics, he replied, referring to the fact that such players were liable for military service, 'If they could die for Italy, then they could play for Italy'.

World Cup, 1930

What was needed, clearly, was an international tournament to which professional teams could be openly admitted; and so the World Cup was born. It was not, in the first instance, much of a success, although the two finalists – Uruguay and Argentina, again – were certainly among the world's best teams. But none of the British countries took part – since they were not members of FIFA, they were not eligible. Other powerful European countries such as Italy, Austria, Germany and Spain stood aside, because the competition was taking place in distant Uruguay; which meant a three-week journey by sea.

The Uruguayans were furious at what they considered

a snub by Europe. But the French went, the Belgians went and the Rumanians went too. In the last case, it certainly helped to have a King so vigorously interested as was King Carol. He not only picked the team himself, but persuaded their various employers to give them time off to go to Uruguay.

The United States of America entered; what is more, they were to reach the semi-final. This is the less surprising when one realizes that, for some years past, the Americans had been making one of their periodic, unsuccessful attempts (the last of them was in 1967) to promote professional soccer. A number of experienced players had been lured across from Britain, and these formed the backbone of the American team. Most of them were big, powerful, heavy men, which prompted the French to nickname them 'The Shot Putters'.

One of the most amusing moments of the tournament occurred when the American trainer rushed on to the field to protest to the referee about a decision with which he disagreed. While he was arguing he dropped his first-aid box, a bottle of chloroform fell out and smashed, and the fumes rose up, making him unconscious. He had to be helped from the field.

Quite how seriously the Uruguayans took the tournament, and football in general, may be judged by the fate of their goalkeeper, Masali. The whole team were staying, secluded, in a large house outside Montevideo, forced to observe a strict curfew. One night, Masali slipped out of the house and into town. On his return, he was caught; and immediately sent home. Despite his fame, despite his achievements in the 1924 and 1928 Olympiads, he did not play a game in the World Cup.

Argentina's team was full of the clever, elusive, fiery players which she would produce in such abundance over the years. Monti, at centre-half, was another kind of typically Argentinian player; a hard man whose tackling was often ruthless to the point of brutality. When France played Argentina, and unluckily lost 1–0, Marcel Pinel, the French centre-half, said that he never came near to Monti without receiving some kind of kick or blow. For the next thirty years and more, the artists would prevail in Argentinian football, but in the late 1960s, a very different kind of football would appear, one based on violence and provocation, resulting in the scandalous World Cup match against England at Wembley in 1966, and the notorious world championship matches between Celtic and Racing Club of Buenos Aires in 1967, and Estudiantes de la Plata and Manchester United in 1968. We shall be meeting Luisito Monti – 'The Man Who Strolls', as he was nicknamed – again; on a very different field.

Argentina beat the United States 6–1 in the semi-final. The tournament had been run in the form of four small, qualifying groups, the winners of each going into the semi-finals. But in an exciting Final, Uruguay ran out the winners, 4–2.

World Cup, 1934

Four years later, it was Italy's turn to stage, and to win, the World Cup. This was a tournament on an altogether larger scale. Now, so many countries wanted to enter that a preliminary, qualifying tournament had to be played – divided into geographical zones – as indeed it still is. On the eve of the competition 'proper', a final qualifying game was played in Rome, when the United States, including several of their doughty British contingent of 1930, defeated Mexico. In years to come, when Mexican football improved and the British had all gone home, it would be Mexico who would consistently bar the way to the United States in World Cup qualifying competitions.

America having come through, sixteen countries were left in the tournament, and now they would play, on the pattern of the F.A. Cup, in a straightforward knock-out tournament. In 1938, the World Cup would follow the same design; but when it was resumed, after the Second World War, the knock-out principle was abandoned. This, as you will see, sometimes led to some rather weird compromises. It has always been hard to know just how to run such an important competition. Ideally, it should be a League championship, stretching over an extended period. This is always the fairest method of assessing the relative strengths of various teams.

But obviously such a competition is quite impossible when international teams are involved. Indeed, if it was hardly practicable in the 1930s, it is still less so now, when so many inter-club competitions have made the clubs less ready and eager to release their players than ever.

The trouble with any tournament which is played over a short period, however, is that luck plays such a large part. A vital player may be injured, and have no time to recover; a fine team may suddenly strike a bad patch. Thus, no one would seriously pretend that Hungary were not the best team, by far and away, in the World Cup of 1954. Yet it was West Germany who won it after Puskas, Hungary's captain and great inside-left, had been injured. More of that, however, in its proper place.

Knock-out tournaments do not really pretend to be fair, except when they are played on the home-and-away, goal aggregate basis with which we have been made familiar by the European Cups. In a sense, their very unfairness and uncertainty is part of their appeal. In what other kinds of contest can David so frequently upset

Goliath, can a Third or Fourth Division team topple a giant from the First Division? On the other hand, it was a little hard on a team which might have travelled thousands of miles to a World Cup to play only a single game before being eliminated.

Italy were determined to win this World Cup. As the celebrated Belgian referee, John Langenus – who always officiated in plus-fours and a cap – said, they made it a little too clear. Mussolini was dictator of Italy at the time; the black-shirted Fascists ruled the country. When England played Italy in Rome and drew 1–1, in 1933, Cliff Bastin, the star of the game and scorer of England's goal, observed that almost every Italian he saw was in uniform.

For Vittorio Pozzo, the exaggerated patriotic spirit of the times was a perfect chance to fire his men with pride and determination. 'Kind but with a strong hand,' was his motto. 'English players,' he once said to me, 'can be handled collectively. Latin players must always be handled individually.' This he did with no small skill.

A French journalist once referred to Pozzo – a journalist himself – as 'the poor captain of a company of millionaires'. That is to say, the Italian players were paid large sums of money, but Pozzo as team manager, or Technical Commissar (*commissario tecnico*) did his job for the love of it.

His players were, as Latin players still are, often very temperamental. When he wanted a man to do something he didn't want to, during a training game, Pozzo would not insist. Instead he would drift slyly up to the player a little later and say, 'You were perfectly right; you *should* do so-and-so', 'so-and-so' being what Pozzo, not the player, had wanted.

Austria were traditionally the great footballing rivals

of Italy. Hugo Meisl told his brother Willy, pessimistically, that Austria were too tired to win the World Cup. As for England – so much for England's pretensions of superiority at the time – he did not think that they would even reach the semi-final. But he did pay tribute to an English footballer. 'If I had one man,' he said, 'I would win the World Cup.' Who, asked his brother, was the man? 'Bastin,' said Hugo.

Italy were not only a fast and clever side, they were also, in the image of Monti, a very tough side; as London would see when they came to play England at Highbury, later that year. They thrashed the United States in Rome without difficulty, but it was a very different matter when they came to play Spain in the beautifully situated stadium in Florence, which lies beneath the tree-covered slopes of Fiesole.

In goal, Spain had Zamora. Fourteen years had passed since he played his first Olympiad, in Antwerp, but – London and 1931 to the contrary – he was as fine and brave a goalkeeper as ever. Though he was severely treated by the Italian forwards, who were seldom restrained by a weak referee, he put up a wonderful performance, enabling his team to hold Italy to a 1–1 draw, after extra time.

Alas, he had been so violently treated that he was unable, at his advanced age for a footballer, to take part in the replay, which took place on the very next day, and Italy won it by the only goal. It was scored by their elegant inside-right, Peppino Meazza, playing his twenty-fifth game for his country. There were no fewer than three Argentinians, Monti, Orsi and the outside-right, Guaita, in the Italian team, and Guaita was to score the only goal of a close semi-final against Austria, played in heavy mud, in Milan. These were hardly the kind of conditions to suit Austria's tall, slim, elegant centre-forward, Mathias Sindelar, nicknamed The Man of Paper.

A kind of latter-day Austrian G. O. Smith, Sindelar was usually a torment to the rugged Monti, who once told Pozzo, 'When I see Sindelar, I see red', and was known to use some pretty obnoxious methods against him.

Uruguay, partly because they were having troubles over professionalism at the time, partly because they were still angry about the European boycott of 'their' World Cup, in 1930, did not send a team to defend the World Cup in 1934. The Argentinians, distressed by the number of players 'stolen' by Italian clubs from their fine 1928 Olympic side, deliberately sent a weakened team; though not a weak one. As for the Brazilians, who went out to Spain, they brought a gifted but slightly disorganized side, which gave Europe its first sight of a great, coloured centre-forward called Leonidas; who would be a hero of the next World Cup.

Negro Footballers

Leonidas, who played in his time for a large number of Brazilian clubs and in Uruguay, too, was a little man, but, in the new fashion of Brazilian Negro footballers, a wonderfully gymnastic player. He had a speciality known as the Aerial Bicycle Kick, which has come to be known since the war as the Scissor Kick, when he would take off from the ground, and while in mid-air kick the ball powerfully over his head at the goal.

The entry of Negro footballers into Brazilian teams was comparatively recent. The Negroes in Brazil had been slaves until late in the previous century, and there was a good deal of prejudice against them. One of the first coloured players, Arthur Friedenreich, generally passed for white, and when he was chosen for the Negro side in a Whites versus Blacks game, he remarked bitterly, 'They are trying to blacken me', Fluminense, the most aristocratic and exclusive of the Rio clubs, held out for years against using Negro players, but eventually had to capitulate, or go under.

For the Negro player, with his wonderful reflexes and his quite original approach to the game, would bring something new not only to Brazilian football, but to the sport at large. If the 1934 and 1938 World Cups had Leonidas, the World Cups of 1958 and the 1960s would give us Pelé, and the wonderful mulatto, Garrincha.

Italy v. Czechoslovakia, 1934

There was to be no South American team in the 1934 Final, however. Italy's opponents were a brave and talented Czech team; there had been a strong tradition of cultured football in Prague since a Scottish international, John Dick, had gone to coach there before the Great War. Shortly before the World Cup, Czechoslovakia, like Hungary, had scored a 2–1 victory over the touring England team. After they had reached the Final, huge quantities of food, and even lucky charms, descended on them from their well-wishers. In the event, they would push Italy very hard indeed.

The match took place in the rather quaint little Stadio Torino, in Rome, just off the famous Via Flaminia. This stadium was pulled down just before the 1960 Olympiad, to give place to an attractive new one called the Stadio Flaminio.

Puc, the outside-left, scored the first goal of the match for the Czechs, who held their lead well into the second half. Orsi at last equalized with a 'fluke' goal, a strange, swerving, dipping shot which went over the head of the fine Czech goalkeeper, Planicka, and dropped under the bar. Just how strange a shot it was may be judged by the fact that when, the following day, he tried to repeat it 'cold' for the benefit of photographers, and with no one in goal, he tried twenty times and couldn't do it. 'We laughed at him,' said Pozzo.

But by then Italy could afford to laugh, because in extra time Schiavio had scored the goal which gave them the World Cup.

The Battle of Highbury

In 1934, the Italian team came to London, to beard the lion in his den. In England, the fact that Italy held the World Cup meant nothing at all; it was no more than a foreign curiosity. How, in any case, could a World Cup be held without England – or Scotland? The Italians, for their part, knew that their position as World Champions could never be fully convincing so long as England stood aloof; unless they could beat England.

It was a Wednesday afternoon international – floodlights were unknown on the football grounds of those days – and a number of England players were injured on the previous Saturday, playing for their clubs. One after another was replaced by an Arsenal man, until the England team consisted of the remarkable number of seven Arsenal players and four others, among them the nineteen-year-old Stanley Matthews, playing his second international, on the right wing.

A minute and a half had barely gone when the incident occurred which was to colour the whole match. Monti limped out of a hard challenge with Ted Drake, the powerful, robust Arsenal and England centre-forward, with a broken toe. To give Monti his due, he wanted to play on, despite the pain, and Pozzo had to employ all

57

his wiles to get him off. When at last he came off, Monti complained, 'He kicked me deliberately', which seemed, to say the least, remarkably unlikely at so early a stage of the game. At all events, the rest of the Italian players believed it, and spent most of the remaining minutes – as they felt – retaliating.

The consequences were atrocious. What could and should have been a game memorable for its skills became one memorable for its brutalities. For twenty minutes, England played splendidly. 'We were playing the best football it was possible to play,' Ted Drake remarked, wonderingly, in later years. 'You couldn't play any better.'

Three goals were scored, even though Ceresoli, Italy's brilliantly acrobatic goalkeeper, saved a penalty by the muscular little English left-winger, Eric Brook of Manchester City. Brook had his revenge by beating Ceresoli with a free kick from outside the penalty area, after Ceresoli had unwisely and arrogantly waved away his colleagues' protecting 'wall'. After that goal, he sat on the ball for a while, and refused to give it up.

There were no substitutes, so Italy had to labour on with their ten men; but as against that, one of their players deliberately smashed an elbow into the face of England's classical left-back and captain, Eddie Hapgood, breaking his nose; and there were many other injuries. No wonder the game has come to be known, in England, as The Battle of Highbury.

But in the second half, the Italian team settled down to play the football of which they were capable. Meazza scored two lovely goals, and only the fine display of the Arsenal goalkeeper, Frank Moss, stopped them equalizing.

Stanley Matthews had a very quiet afternoon; you could hardly blame him. In the years, the many years, that followed, Matthews was to prove to those who criticized him that day that he had a wonderful flair for the great occasion. He played till he was fifty in League football, ending his career, as he had begun it, with Stoke City, after a long and dazzling interlude with Blackpool. Pale and relatively fragile in appearance, he was another great star who did not, when static, look much like a footballer. In motion, he was unique and superb.

Above all, he had an astonishing body swerve. Full-backs everywhere knew about it, but they could seldom if ever do anything to counter it. Out on the right wing, where he lurked in wait for the ball, and his prey, Matthews would sway to the left, drawing the full-back with him, off balance, then snap to the right, pulling the ball away with the outside of his right foot. This done, his acceleration was remarkable. You could never catch him.

Time and again Matthews was dropped from the England team because his methods were considered too unorthodox. After the war, with the return of the immensely talented Preston outside-right, Tom Finney, from Army service, the selectors had a ready-made excuse to leave out Matthews. But sometimes, when Matthews played on one wing, Tom Finney on the other, the result was exquisite football: as in 1947, when England beat Portugal 10–0 in Lisbon, or the following year, when they defeated Italy 4–0 in Turin; and the Italians behaved like angels. (It was to be Pozzo's last match in charge of them.)

Wembley was often the stage for Matthews' finest performances, such as in 1953, when, seeing his last possibility of a Cup winners' medal gliding away from him, he exerted all his powers to master Bolton's defence, and wrest Blackpool a 4–3 victory. Or, again, in 1956, when he was recalled once more to the England team, at the age of 41, to tantalize, torment and generally outplay Nilton Santos of Brazil, one of the best left-backs of his epoch.

Besides all this, Matthews was an impeccable sportsman. When he was fouled, he would not deign to retaliate. If a free kick was given against him, it was such an unusual event as to demand a paragraph in that evening's football editions of the newspapers.

There was serious talk, after the Battle of Highbury, of giving up all matches against foreign countries, but luckily it came to nothing. It was bad enough that England did not compete for World Cups; it would have been still more serious had they cut themselves off in splendid isolation altogether.

So they continued to repel the foreign challenge at home, getting six goals against Hungary in 1936, again at Arsenal Stadium, thrashing the Rest of Europe there, 3–0, in 1938; and to lose occasional matches, abroad. In 1936, Hugo Meisl, lying almost on the Austrian goal netting in the last phases of play, finally had the satisfaction of seeing Austria beat England 2–1, in Vienna.

In 1938, England won a splendid victory in Berlin, annihilating Germany 6–3, after being forced by timorous diplomats and officials to give the Nazi salute. The Germans, who had been in training camp in the Black Forest, were desperate to win, to prove their 'superiority' over the supposedly decadent English; but they were thoroughly outclassed, and Matthews had another marvellous game.

Later in 1938, Germany, under the team management of the wily Sepp Herberger – under whom they would win the 1954 World Cup – competed in the third World Cup, in France. They were quickly knocked out by little Switzerland, who had just defeated the very England team that won in Berlin.

Italy retained the trophy, using only two of the players with whom they had won it in 1934: the inside-forwards, Meazza and Ferrari. They had discovered a fine, powerful new centre-forward in Silvio Piola, dangerous with head, foot – and even fist, as England were to discover in Milan, the following year. Lashing out over his shoulder, Piola punched into the England net a ball he could not otherwise reach, and the German referee, Dr Pecos Bauwens, gave a goal. It took England all their time to equalize. To add insult to injury, Piola followed through and caught George Male, the England right-back, in the eye; though, as Male was always at pains to point out, it was an accident.

1938 was a notable World Cup for centre-forwards, for there were also Leonidas of Brazil, Dr George Sarosi, a learned and skilful Hungarian, and a big, fair-haired Norwegian called Brunyldsen, who frightened Italy terribly in their first, close match in Marseilles. Later Pozzo was to call him, 'a cruel thorn in my crown of roses'. Austria, who had just been overrun by the Germans, did not compete; nor did Spain, who were in the toils of civil war. Argentina and Uruguay were both absent, and it was left to the brilliant but explosive Brazilians to defend the prestige of South American football.

This, on the whole, they did very well, though their players ran amok in a violent game against the Czechs, in which Nejedly, Czechoslovakia's gifted inside-left –

'pure as Bohemian glass', a French writer called him – had his leg broken. Pozzo thought Domingas Da Guia, Brazil's poised full-back, the best in the tournament; but even Da Guia lost his temper and was sent off. In the later 1960s, his son, Ademir, became a star midfield player for Palmeiras of Sao Paolo – and for Brazil.

The inside-forward trio was splendid, Leonidas receiving particularly fine support from Tim, who is still prominent in South American football today as a manager. He has been successful in both Brazil and Argentina. To this very day, it is a mystery why Brazil should have left out both these celebrated forwards in their semifinal match against Italy. They were both perfectly fit; and the only stated explanation, that Brazil were confidently saving them for the Final, still seems outrageous. At all events, there was to be no Final for Brazil. The Italians won, then made short work of Hungary. 4–2 was the score, and Italy had shown again that you could still achieve excellent results, still build an outstanding and effective team, without having recourse to the W formation and the stopper centre-half.

The England team with which they drew in 1939 was a fine one; one which had just beaten Scotland in Glasgow for the first time for years. They would not play another full international there till 1948; while the World Cup would disappear under Jules Rimet's bed, not to be played for again till 1950.

5. England's Lost Horizon

Wartime Football

With the outbreak of war, official tournaments were suspended in Britain. There would be no F.A. Cup till 1946, no Football League or International Championship till the season after that.

Yet during the war years England for a while had a very fine team, won complete superiority over Scotland for the first time, and perhaps had as many great players as at any time in the past, or in the future.

Teamwork was certainly helped by the fact that most professional footballers went into the Army or Royal Air Force Physical Training Corps, and played regularly together in the Services representative teams. Many of the Army footballers, in fact, played club football together week by week – for little Aldershot. The practice of allowing 'guest' players – borrowed from other teams – to be used permitted Aldershot, a Third Division club in peace-time, to call on the wealth of talent employed at the local Army Physical Training School. So there were days on which Aldershot could choose the complete England half-back line, Cliff Britton and Joe Mercer of Everton as wing-halves, Stanley Cullis of the Wolves at centre-half, behind a forward-line led by the rampant young Tommy Lawton, also of Everton, and marshalled by Jimmy Hagan, the shrewd England and Sheffield United inside-left.

The only internationals which took place were between England and Scotland and between England and Wales, who played one another several times a season. Wales did not play Scotland, and Ireland, for obvious reasons, could not be included. German submarines could lurk in the Irish Sea.

With Stanley Matthews, who was in the R.A.F., at last winning a regular place in the England team, and making up a superb partnership with his fellow-R.A.F. player, Raich Carter of Sunderland, with the strapping Lawton heading and shooting goals, with the towering Frank Swift, of Manchester City, as safe as he was spectacular in goal, there was no holding England. Once, they actually beat Scotland 8–0 at Maine Road, Manchester. Lawton hooked one ball over his head and into the net while sitting with his back to the goal. Yet Scotland at that time were by no means without good players; excellent wing-halves such as Bill Shankly and Matt Busby, known nowadays as the managers of Liverpool and Manchester United, but then playing, respectively, for Preston North End and Liverpool. Busby, in fact, never actually played for Manchester United, but for their Mancunian rivals, Manchester City, who sold him to Liverpool shortly before the war.

Wales, in fact, had rather more success against England than the Scots. They even beat them at Wembley in 1940. Inspired by their famous and remarkable Secretary, Ted Robbins, they had for years risen above themselves

1. above: **Lord Kinnaird,** President of the Football Association 1890 to 1923. A pioneer of the game, who figured in several Cup Finals for Wanderers and the Old Etonians. (*Radio Times Hulton Picture Library*)

2. below: The England XI of 1895. Three great forwards, **Billy Bassett, Steve Bloomfer** and **John Goodall** sit from left to right in the front row. **'Pa' Jackson,** founder of the Corinthians, wearing a cricket cap, at the left of the back row. (*Radio Times Hulton Picture Library*)

3. **G. O. Smith,** arguably the most gifted of all English centre-
forwards, though he was averse to heading the ball. Played for
Old Carthusians, Corinthians, and many times for England
between 1894 and 1900. (*Radio Times Hulton Picture Library*)

4. left: **Johnny Goodall,** the Preston North End and England
centre-forward, and outstanding member of the Preston
'Invincibles' who won Cup and League last century. (*Radio Times
Hulton Picture Library*)

5. right: **Hughie Gallagher,** tiny Scottish international centre-
forward who brilliantly led the attacks of Newcastle, Chelsea and
his country between the wars. (*Radio Times Hulton Picture Library*)

6. below: **Charlie Buchan,** inventor of the third back game. A
brilliant inside-forward who left Arsenal as an amateur, made
his name with Sunderland, then returned to Arsenal in 1925 in the
famous 'hundred pounds a goal' transfer. (*Radio Times Hulton
Picture Library*)

7. right: **Matt Busby,** as a
Manchester City wing-half,
just before he helped them
win the 1934 Cup Final. The
celebrated Manchester
United manager was a fine
player, who captained Scotland
during the war. (*Radio Times
Hulton Picture Library*)

8. below: **Dixie Dean,** Everton's
powerful centre-forward
in the late twenties and early
thirties. He scored 60 First
Division goals in one season,
1927–8. (*Radio Times Hulton
Picture Library*)

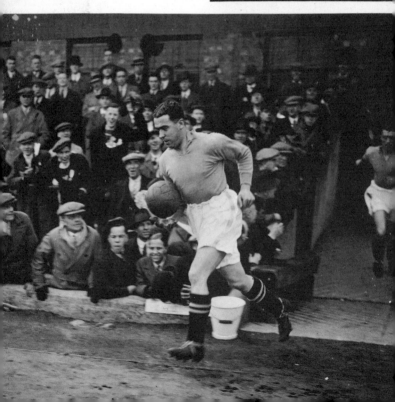

9. **Tommy Lawton** at 19. The photograph, taken in 1938, shows Lawton in the colours of Everton, with whom he won a Championship medal. He was a magnificent successor to Dean and played many times for England. (*Radio Times Hulton Picture Library*)

10. opposite: **Wilf Mannion** of Middlesbrough and England, an outstanding inside-forward of the years 1938 to 1950. (*Topix*)

11. left: **Joe Mercer,** shown as an Everton and England left-half, 1944. He didn't retire until 1954, when he broke a leg as captain of Arsenal. Later he became a celebrated manager. (*Radio Times Hulton Picture Library*)

12. below: **F.A. CUP FINAL** 1950. **Denis Compton** plays on Arsenal's left-wing at Wembley. The challenger is Liverpool's centre-half **Laurie Hughes**, who later went to Brazil to play in the World Cup. (*Topix*)

13. **Alf Ramsey** as a player; he was an outstandingly cool, creative right-back with Spurs and England. (*Radio Times Hulton Picture Library*)

14. above: **Stan Mortensen** and **Stanley Matthews,** a splendid right-wing for England and Blackpool in the late forties and early fifties. (*Topix*)

15. below: Wembley, November 1953. Lambs to the slaughter. An unsuspecting **Billy Wright** leads out the England team which lost their unbeaten home record 6–3 to Hungary, led by **Ferenc Puskas**. The goalkeeper, **Gyula Grosics**, follows him. (*Topix*)

16. above: **Bobby** and **Jackie Charlton,** brothers and colleagues in England jerseys, rivals with Manchester United and Leeds United. (*Topix*)

17. below: **Manchester United,** 1958. The 'Busby Babes' who came to so tragic an end in the Munich air disaster. Back row (left to right): Edwards, Foulkes, Jones, Wood, Colman, Pegg; front row: Berry, Whelan, Byrne, Taylor, Viollet. (*Topix*)

18. A happy **Bobby Moore** holds up the World Cup, which his England team has just won. 1966. (*Topix*)

19. **Eusebio** scores his second goal for Portugal in the 1966 World Cup match against Bulgaria. (*Press Association Photos*)

20. above: World Cup 1966. **Geoff Hurst,** playing his first
World Cup match for England, brilliantly heads the goal which
beat Argentina in the Wembley quarter-final. (*Topix*)

21. below: World Cup Final, Wembley 1966. **Weber,** on the
far left, equalizes for West Germany against England, seconds
before the final whistle, beating **Ray Wilson** to the ball. **Seeler** and
Schnellinger are the other German players, **Gordon Banks** sprawls
on the ground, **Bobby Moore** raises an appealing hand. (*Topix*)

22. F.A. Cup Final, Wembley 1969. **Francis Lee**, the England and Manchester City forward, fails to penetrate the Leicester City defence. (*Topix*)

23. **Jimmy Greaves** shoots past **Yeats** (right) to score Tottenham Hotspurs' first goal in their match against Liverpool, 1968. (*United Press International*)

24. **George Best** of Manchester United and Northern Ireland, a forward whose exciting skills made him one of the most renowned sportsmen of his time. (*D. Green*)

25. An action picture of **Johann Cruyff** of Holland. (*Topix*)

on the international field. Twice in the latter 1930s they actually won the British Championship, for all the power of the English and the Scots.

Ted Robbins

Ted Robbins had that magical gift, shared by Chapman, Pozzo and Hugo Meisl, of inspiring his players, of making them play far above themselves. This was just as well, since Wales, like Ireland, had serious difficulties then in getting the players they wanted. The English Football League clubs, for whom practically all the Welsh and most of the Irish internationals played, were not obliged to release them, even for mid-week games. On the occasion of one of these – in Scotland – poor Robbins found himself so short of men that he had to choose three who played for clubs outside the Football League; yet Wales held Scotland to a draw. Quite ordinary players would pull on the red Welsh jersey and become heroes for a brief afternoon.

'Come on!' Robbins would tell a shy, new player. 'Get your feet under the table. I'll be your Daddy!' It was in this friendly, family atmosphere that Welsh football flourished.

Blackpool

The first few years of the war were also the last years of Arsenal's greatness. Their fine team slowly fell apart; and they were given a warning in 1943. Having just won the wartime League South Cup Final by thrashing Charlton Athletic 7–1 at Wembley, they were well beaten, 4–2, by the Northern Cup-winners, Blackpool. Stanley Matthews, then playing for Blackpool as a guest,

though he was sold to them by Stoke City in 1947, turned
the Arsenal defence inside out.

Stan Mortensen

The finest of Blackpool's recent 'discoveries' did not play
for them that day; he could not win a place against such
star 'guests' as Ronnie Dix, of Tottenham Hotspur. His
name was Stanley Mortensen, he came from the North-
East, and his first appearance in an international match
was, curiously enough, for Wales. He was reserve to
England in a match at Wembley when a Welsh player
was injured, and England sportingly allowed Mortensen
to take his place.

Mortensen was soon playing for the full English international team. Although, as a boy player, he was criticized for being slow, his wonderful acceleration became
one of his chief weapons. He was to score many fine
goals for England. Three of them turned a difficult match
against Sweden at Highbury in 1947, which England
would otherwise have lost. Four had gone into the Portuguese net in Lisbon, the previous summer.

But perhaps the most extraordinary of all his goals,
one they still speak about in Italy, was scored in Turin,
the following year. The ball was almost on the goal-line
when Mortensen caught it and, with an astonishing high,
right-footed shot, beat a goalkeeper who had advanced
from his goal, convinced that there could be no danger.
England went on to win 4–0. Mortensen's courage on the
field was equalled by his courage off it, for he had to
fight his way back from an aeroplane crash – a training
flight in an R.A.F. bomber – in which he was badly
injured.

International Football

With the end of the war, England at last rejoined FIFA, the international association, and so once more – together with Scotland, Wales and Ireland – became eligible to play in the World Cup.

To celebrate this return, a match was arranged in May, 1947, between Great Britain and the Rest of Europe, at Hampden Park. Great Britain won it very easily, by six goals to one, Wilf Mannion, the blond Middlesbrough and England inside-forward, having a particularly fine game. The European team, which included players from ten different countries, never really found a common language, though Gunnar Nordahl, the big Swedish centre-forward, who would become a famous name even in Britain before he was done, did equalize the first English goal.

Coaching

British football, however, was tending to stand still. The warnings of Jimmy Hogan and his kind had gone unheard. Coaching was still discouraged, was still regarded as something fit for foreigners rather than Britons; though the Football Association had set up an ambitious and lively coaching scheme.

Over this there presided a former Manchester United centre-half and physical education teacher called Walter Winterbottom. He was also appointed to the position of team manager of the English international side; the first England had ever had. A tall, courteous, intelligent, likeable man, Winterbottom remained the English team manager till Alf Ramsey succeeded him in 1963; but two such demanding jobs were surely too much to give any one man. Winterbottom took the England team to four

World Cups, but it never got beyond the quarter-finals.

Manchester United

The new force in English football was to be Manchester United; despite the fact that for several years after the war they did not even have a ground of their own. Old Trafford had been badly bombed during the war, and United were obliged to share Maine Road with their neighbours and rivals, Manchester City.

Between the wars United had been a pretty undistinguished club, which had had long spells in the Second Division. Its great past lay away back, before the Great War, when players like Billy Meredith and the illustrious half-back line of Duckworth, Roberts and Bell had made it a force. The appointment as manager of Matt Busby was to change all that.

Busby, as we have seen, had been an excellent wing-half-back with Manchester City – where he won a Cup medal – and Liverpool; a clever, thoughtful player in the Scottish tradition. He had been brought up in the mining town of Bellshill, which had already produced those two remarkable forwards, Hughie Gallacher and Alex James. Busby may have taken over a club with no ground of its own, but he was fortunate enough to inherit some very fine players. Some, like the forwards Jack Rowley and Stan Pearson, the mature defender, Johnny Carey, who captained the Rest of Europe against Great Britain, had been pre-war League players. Others, such as Johnny Morris, the lively little inside-right, John Aston, at full-back, and Henry Cockburn, the tiny left-half, had come forward in the last stages of the war.

In 1948, United had their first success, beating Blackpool 4–2 in the Cup Final. When they found themselves a goal down, Johnny Carey, their skipper, calmly passed round the message, 'Keep on playing football'. United did; to score three goals in a row.

The story goes that when Herbert Chapman was dying, early in 1934, he told George Allison, his successor as Arsenal's manager, 'The team's played out, Mr Allison. We must rebuild.' Arsenal did, to fine effect; but few clubs have rebuilt with such regularity and such extraordinary success as Busby and Manchester United; none has so triumphantly survived disaster.

Munich Air Crash

In May, 1949, an aeroplane carrying the Italian champions, Torino, including eight current Italian internationals, back from a tour of Portugal, crashed on a hill above the city at Superga, killing all seventeen players. Torino, who were in the process of winning their fifth successive Championship, have never since finished in the top three.

In 1958, at Munich airport, an Elizabethan airliner carrying the brilliant young Manchester United team back from a European Cup-tie in Belgrade hit a building at the end of the runway and crashed, killing eight of the United team, a number of journalists, including Frank Swift, and very severely injuring Busby himself. Among the dead players were Geoff Byrne, England's left-back, Tommy Taylor, the England centre-forward, and Duncan Edwards, the massive, twenty-two-year-old England left-half, considered one of the finest young players of his generation. Other players, such as Jackie Blanchflower, the clever Irish international centre-half, younger brother of Tottenham's Danny, were never to play again.

That would have been the end of most clubs as a force, but it was not the end of United. Busby, who had fashioned his so-called 'Babes' as resplendent successors to the Rowley–Pearson–Carey team, fought his way back to health, then built up yet another fine team, the symbol of which would be a young survivor of the crash, the fair-haired Bobby Charlton.

Matt Busby

Busby himself was one of the earlier 'track-suited' managers. That is to say, he believed in his first years as a manager in the importance of putting on a track suit and going out to coach and train with the players. This is so commonly done today that it seems nothing unusual; but until well into the 1950s, the normal British manager was never seen on the football field. He shut himself away in his office, leaving the preparation of his players to his bucket and sponge man, the trainer. The trainer's usual method of preparation, as we have seen, was to send them pounding around the track. Training with the ball, which might seem to any reasonable person the very essence of preparing for football, was largely unknown.

George Raynor

Many of the best British coaches continued to work abroad, training foreign teams to beat us. Among them was George Raynor, a little Yorkshireman who had been a modest outside-right with such clubs as Rotherham and Aldershot before the war, driving a coal lorry during the summer to make ends meet.

During the war, he suddenly found himself coaching the national team of Iraq, in the Middle East, and, after it was over, the Football Association recommended him to become national coach of Sweden.

Sweden

The Swedes, who had kept out of the war, had some outstandingly good footballers at the time, among them the three Nordahl brothers, Gunnar, Bertil and Knud; Nils Liedholm, a splendid inside-forward, and Gunnar Gren, a clever inside-right. All these would eventually play in Italy. Gunnar Nordahl, Gren and Liedholm for years made up an inside-forward trio for Milan which was nicknamed *Grenoli*, after their respective surnames.

Nobody in Sweden had heard of Raynor, and he met some rather acid criticism in the newspapers. But he soon won everybody on to his side by working out a plan to 'spring' Switzerland's complicated defence, in his first international match, explaining it in advance to the journalists; and succeeding. Sweden won.

His excellent team won the Olympic tournament in 1948, at Wembley. Then, even when so many of his best players had left Sweden to turn professional abroad, he was still able to build a side which took third place in the World Cup of 1950, in Brazil. Much later, after a spell in Italy, he returned to Sweden to take charge of a 1958 World Cup side which included Liedholm and Gren. 'We're the slowest team in the competition,' he said, cheerfully. 'If there was a relay race, Sweden would finish last. But we'll still reach the Final.' So, as we shall see, they did.

World Cup, 1950

England were the only British team to travel to the 1950 World Cup; which was the measure of Scotland's strange insularity. The British International Tournament was designated as a qualifying group for the World Cup from which – most generously – the first and second teams

71

would both qualify for Brazil. Scotland arrogantly said that they would go only if they won the title. In the last match of the British competition, they met, as usual, England – at Hampden Park – and unluckily lost by the only goal.

Roy Bentley of Chelsea, the first of the so-called 'deep lying' centre-forwards, scored for England. Willy Bauld, the Scots centre-forward, beat Williams, in the England goal, but his shot came back from the bar. Billy Wright, England's exuberant young captain, begged George Young, the towering captain of Scotland, to persuade his officials to change their minds; but they would not. England went to Brazil alone.

They went, alas, without their centre-half, Neil Franklin of Stoke City, who had suddenly flown off to Bogota, Colombia, in South America, to play for a club called Milionarios. Colombia at the time were outside FIFA, and for some years past had been luring the best Argentinian players. Franklin was reported to be earning £50 a week, as compared with the wretched £14 a week, the maximum wage permitted to an English professional. Though the fixed, maximum wage slowly went up to £20, it was not till 1961 that the players, splendidly led by the Chairman of the Professional Footballers' Association, Jimmy Hill, threw off the yoke, and the 'maximum' was belatedly abolished.

Yet even without Franklin, England had a very good team, and the disaster which awaited them was hardly apparent. They had Billy Wright, Stanley Mortensen, Wilf Mannion, Tom Finney. They had the solid Alf Ramsey, nicknamed at Tottenham 'The General', at right-back. They had even, at the last moment, repented their folly and recalled Stanley Matthews, who had been on tour with a Football Association party in North America.

For this World Cup, the teams were divided, as in 1930, into small qualifying groups. Unfortunately a number of withdrawals had seriously unbalanced these. Some teams, like England, had to play three matches in a four-team group. Others, such as the eventual winners, Uruguay, had a much easier passage. The Uruguayans, indeed, had only one match to play before reaching the four-team final pool: an 8–0 trot against Bolivia, the weakest side in the whole competition.

Brazil's passion for football surprised their English visitors. A new stadium, the Maracana, had been built, capable of taking 200,000 spectators; twice the size of Wembley, and much larger than the largest stadium in Britain, Hampden Park. With their chants, their samba rhythms, and their habit of burning hundreds of newspapers or waving thousands of handkerchiefs at the end of a game, the Brazilian crowds were something quite new to the majority of the English players; though Ramsey, on tour with Southampton, had been there before.

England

England played in a group with Chile, the United States and Spain. With Brazil, they were joint favourites to win the tournament. Italy, the holders, had still to recover from the terrible Superga crash; though their very clever team had given England an awful shock in the fog at Tottenham, the previous November, losing 2–0 a match they would have won, without Bert Williams's superlative goalkeeping.

England played and won their first match in Rio, beating Chile 2–0 without much distinction. Then they flew north to a town called Belo Horizonte – Beautiful Horizon – to play the United States. On the face of it, they could scarcely have had easier opposition. The Americans asked one English reporter whether he had brought a cribbage board along, to keep the score. Their team was captained by a right-half called Eddie McIlvenny, a Scot who, eighteen months previously, had been released with a free transfer by Wrexham, the English Third Division club. Larry Gaetjens, the centre-forward who would score the vital and even historic goal, was a Haitian. The team manager, Bill Jeffreys, was a Scot who had come out many years before to the United States to work on the railway, had played football against the Penn State team, been invited to the university to become their coach, and had stayed there ever since.

The ground was small – Belo Horizonte's present, majestic stadium lay far in the future – the dressing-room accommodation so primitive that the England team, who had stayed in a nearby, British-owned gold mine, preferred to change in their hotel.

From the first, they overran the American team, but the fine goalkeeping of Borghi, the sturdy defence of Colombo, a centre-half who played in gloves, some inaccurate finishing and some bad luck, prevented them from scoring before half-time.

In the second half, the unthinkable happened; America scored. Bahr, the left-half, hit a long ball into the England goalmouth. Gaetjens, the centre-forward, stooped to it, and deflected it past Bert Williams. For all their frantic, subsequent efforts, England still could not score. America beat them, 1–0.

Any chance the shaken English team had of surviving disappeared when they lost their last match, in Rio, 1–0 against Spain; though they were a little unfortunate to be beaten. Home they went, leaving the field to the four group winners, Brazil, Uruguay, Sweden and Spain.

74

Sweden

Sweden, in their first match, had surprised and defeated Italy in Sao Paolo. The Italians took 'revenge' by buying up almost the whole of the Swedish side as soon as the World Cup was over. The hero of that match was a vigorous centre-forward called Hans Jeppson who, before he answered the lure of Italy – and the Naples club – played very successfully for Charlton Athletic in the First Division. Among his achievements was the scoring of a hat-trick at Arsenal, against a young goalkeeper playing his first League game: Jack Kelsey, later to become a famous Welsh international.

Jeppson was supported, in the Swedish team, by two clever little inside-forwards, Kalle Palmer and Nacka Skoglund; of whom Skoglund would play very successfully in Italy for many years for Internazionale of Milan. When the team had a training game in Rio before the World Cup began, Palmer and Skoglund enjoyed themselves with some skilful dribbling and inter-passing. But when they went to Raynor afterwards for praise, they received instead a sound telling-off. In future, he ordered them, they must be much more direct and less fanciful. The orders were taken to heart.

Brazil and Uruguay

Brazil made a somewhat awkward start in the competition, beating an excellent Yugoslav team with difficulty, and were held to a draw by Switzerland, in Sao Paolo.

In the Final Pool, however – which, like the eliminating matches, was played like a miniature league, rather than on a knock-out basis – they suddenly took wing. Their brilliant inside-forward trio of Zizinho, Ademir and Jair, cleverly supported by the attacking right-half,

75

Bauer, tore first the Spanish then the Swedish defences to pieces at the Maracana, scoring first six then seven goals, against a mere one in reply. Marvellous ball-players, admirably quick both in thought and movement, deadly dangerous anywhere near goal, the Brazilian inside-forwards seemed quite irresistible. Uruguay scraped through rather luckily against Sweden, drew with Spain, and seemed quite certain to give up, in their final match against Brazil, the one point the home country needed to win the title.

Not that the Brazilians were over-confident. 'The Uru-guayans,' said their manager, Flavio Costa, 'have always been a bogey team to us.' Neither side played the third back game. The Uruguayans, indeed, depended heavily on their roaming centre-half, the giant Varela, while Brazil played something that they called the Diagonal System. Bauer, the right-half, played the customary, middle of the field game of a W formation wing-half; but Bigode, the other, marked the opposing outside-right, in the manner of an 'old school' wing-half. Danilo, the centre-half, was an attacking player. The trouble with the diagonal system was that it tended to leave the full-back or half-back marking the winger rather unprotected; a weakness which would cost Brazil two goals and the World Cup.

You will see that several of the Brazilians were called not by their surnames, as is the custom in Britain and most of Europe, but by their Christian names; or even, in some cases, by nicknames. Pelé, Didì and Garrincha were later examples of this. Garrincha's name meant 'A Little Bird'. This had long been a habit in Brazil, where the players sometimes assumed the strangest names. One called himself JAHU, after the initials on the first aero-plane he ever flew in; he even took out his teeth and had them embossed with the letters. Another called himself by the number of a winning lottery ticket; while in 1969, Brazil made use of a goalkeeper nicknamed Picasso. Their 1958 World Cup centre-forward – for the opening games – was nicknamed Mazzola, because he looked rather like Valentino Mazzola, the famous captain of Italy who died in the Torino air crash. When, after that World Cup, he was transferred to Milan, he was called by his proper name, José Altafini, because Mazzola's son Sandrino was by then a young player with Internazionale.

But to return to the game. Brazil attacked feverishly all through the first half, but simply couldn't penetrate a Uruguayan defence in which Maspoli, in goal, Varela and the little coloured half-back, Andrade – nephew of the Andrade who played in the 1930 Cup-winning team – were outstanding.

Immediately after half-time, Friaca, the outside-right, scored for Brazil, and the Maracana erupted in a tumult of joy. But the Uruguayans had taken the measure of the Brazilians by now, and they were far from beaten. Inspired by Varela, who started now to move forward, rather than back, they maintained a series of sharp, economical breakaways which frequently had Brazil's defence in trouble.

At last from one of them Juan Schiaffino, the tall, pale Uruguayan inside-left, a superb ball-player and passer of a ball, took a pass from Chico Ghiggia, his little outside-right, and equalized. Ghiggia himself, late in the game, sped past Bigode to score with a powerful shot which gave Uruguay the match, and their second World Cup.

No wonder Ondino Viera, Uruguay's 1966 World Cup manager, was to say, 'Other countries have their history. We have our football.'

6. The Marvellous Hungarians

Somehow or other, as they say in boxing, England rode the punch, and managed to persuade themselves that their shocking defeat by the United States was not important. True, it was a freak. 'If we'd played them again,' said Laurie Hughes, the young Liverpool centre-half who took Franklin's place, 'we'd have hammered them easy.' So nothing really changed. Footballers in Britain still kept thumping round the track, instead of practising with the ball: until, in November, 1953, the Hungarians came.

Hungary

Their team had been carefully built up in Eastern Europe, behind the Iron Curtain, for several years, before it started to play matches outside it. In common with a number of Communist countries, Hungary put the national team first, the clubs a very distant second. So it was that, when an outstanding player appeared, he was often as not transferred to the army club, Honved, which had been formed at the end of the war. Puskas and Kocsis, the two splendid, goal-scoring Hungarian inside-forwards, were both with Honved. So was the attacking right-half, Josef Boszik, a member of the Hungarian Parliament. The only celebrated player in the side who stayed with his own club was the deep-lying centre-forward, Nandor Hidegkuti, of Red Banner, Voros Logobo, who in 1956, after the Hungarian uprising against Russian occupation, changed to their original name of MTK.

Shortly before the Hungarians came to London, to attack England's unbeaten home record against foreign teams, they were held to a draw by Sweden in Budapest: 2–2. The credit, as so often, belonged largely to little George Raynor, who saw that the Hungarians pivoted on Hidegkuti, and marked him closely – with his centre-forward in one half, his inside-left in the other. 'If you win,' Raynor told his Swedes, 'I'll paint Stalin's moustache [on the memorial] red!'

England, unfortunately, were seldom noted for the intelligence of their tactics, till Alf Ramsey became manager. More, they were especially open to the clever central thrusts of Hungary, because they were still looking for a centre-half to follow Franklin. Hungary were especially clever at drawing the stopper centre-half out of position. Sometimes it was the stocky Ferenc Puskas, with his ferocious left-foot shot, who would go through, sometimes the clever Sandor Kocsis – known as Golden Head for his heading skill – sometimes Hidegkuti himself.

Indeed, it was Hidegkuti who was the great star of Hungary's victory over England. He scored the first goal after only ninety seconds, skilfully drawing Harry Johnston, the England centre-half – a converted wing-half – out of position with a swerve, then hitting the ball through the gap.

England, whose team was as hastily thrown together as Hungary's was well knit and experienced, fought well in the first half; but it was largely a question of desperate individual bursts. Two of them, by Jackie Sewell and Stan Mortensen, brought goals, but the intelligence, the speed of thought and movement, and the unexpected striking power of the Hungarians were too much for England. After half-time, Hungary quickly built their lead to 5–2 – the fifth goal was put in by their right-half, Boszik – and ran out winners, eventually, by 6–3. England's third goal was scored from the penalty spot by Alf Ramsey.

Training

At last English football woke up to the fact that it had been surpassed; even if, for a time, it drew all sorts of mistaken conclusions. For a while, the accent seemed to be placed on quantity rather than quality; what was wrong, it was mistakenly believed, was that English footballers did not train hard enough. Watford, a Third Division club then, decided to bring its players back for extra, afternoon training. The truth, needless to say, was not that English footballers did not do enough training but that the training which they did was wrong.

However, the way was clear at last to new ideas, to a realization that we had fallen far behind the Continent in many ways. The door was open to the products of Walter Winterbottom's revolution in coaching, to the track-suited manager who in the years to come would more and more frequently replace the desk-bound manager who never came out to train. Ball practice at last began to replace the dreary, unimaginative training which had put stamina first at the expense of skill.

World Cup, 1954

Yet the Hungarians did not win the 1954 World Cup; even if they were far and away the best team in it. What a strange and faintly tragic story that is, as one looks back on it. If Puskas had not had his own way, and had been left out of the Final, Hungary would surely have won. But that, as they say, is football.

England

Shortly before the World Cup began, in Switzerland, England had been still more thoroughly demolished in Budapest, by 7–1. You would have thought that they would have learned something from their defeat at Wembley, that they would at least come out with some form of a defensive plan. Not a bit of it. Their team – once again thrown haphazardly together at the last moment – played without any obvious trace of a plan at all, and paid a heavy penalty.

When England got to Switzerland, they once again did what they should have done before – recalled Stanley Matthews, and once again his splendid performances put them to shame. He was splendid in their opening match against Belgium, operating largely in the middle, as a constructive player, rather than out on the wing. Sloppy mistakes resulted in England being held to a draw, just as Gilbert Merrick's goalkeeping mistakes would lead to their elimination by Uruguay in the quarter-finals. Quite how Merrick kept his place after his performance against Hungary at Wembley was another of the many mysteries which, till Ramsey's coming, surrounded English team selection.

Still, at least one good thing came out of that World Cup; England at last found a decent centre-half. When Sid Owen, the Luton centre-half, was hurt, Billy Wright moved from wing-half to take his place, so efficiently that he stayed there for years.

This World Cup, which was perhaps the last to be distinguished by open, attractive, attacking football, was organized in the most absurd way; a way both complicated and contradictory. In each four-team group, two teams were 'seeded', as in a lawn tennis tournament. Neither met the other; they played two matches against the unseeded teams, and if these ended in a draw at full-time, extra time was automatically played, to get a result. If two teams were level on points at the completion of the group's matches, they played off.

West Germany and Hungary

Thus it was that West Germany, entering their first World Cup since the war (they had previously been barred from FIFA), were able to throw away an eliminating match 8–3 to Hungary, then go on to beat the Hungarians in the Final. This was possible because the Germans, having beaten Turkey once, knew that they could beat them again whenever they cared to. Sepp Herberger, wiliest of team managers, therefore deliberately put out a weak team against Hungary. It might be said that the kick which won the World Cup was that with which Werner Liebrich, the German centre-half, lamed Puskas.

Puskas did not play in Hungary's next two matches; yet the Hungarians were just as dangerous in attack without him. Zoltan Czibor, the left-winger, moved inside to take his place. Brazil were beaten 4–2 in a notorious quarter-final; Uruguay fell 4–2 in a magnificent semi-final.

The Brazilian game, alas, turned into a battle, in which three players, two Brazilians and a Hungarian, were sent off by the English referee, Arthur Ellis, and the Brazilians afterwards invaded the Hungarian dressing-room. A great pity, because both sides were capable of exceptional play. Brazil had an outside-right in Julinho who was one of the finest ever to grace a World Cup, powerful, fast, unusually clever on the ball. He scored a spectacular goal.

The semi-final against Uruguay went to extra time. The Uruguayans, who had beaten England 4–2 despite a spate of injuries, and had previously walked over a feeble Scottish team, 7–0, eventually fell to Kocsis's heading ability. Juan Hohberg, a naturalized Argentinian, scored both their goals, and Schiaffino again showed what a fine player he was. Hohberg would become team manager of the 1970 World Cup side.

The West Germans, captained very shrewdly from inside-forward by the thirty-three-year-old Fritz Walter, a former paratrooper, got better and better as the tournament wore on. They hadn't the brilliance of Hungary, or the novelty of play, but their defence was extremely solid, they were physically very strong, and in their big, strong outside-right, Helmut Rahn, they had the man who would eventually win them the Final.

They easily beat Turkey in the play-off, narrowly won against yet another excellent Yugoslav team in the quarter-finals, and annihilated Austria 6–1 in the semi-final. Walter Zeman, Austria's well-known goalkeeper, had a mysteriously poor game, and not even Ernst

Ocwirk, their superb half-back, could plug the many holes in the defence. Ocwirk, who had made his famous name in Europe as an attacking centre-half, was now playing wing-half. Austria – like Brazil – had at last turned to the third-back game. It was the death knell of the old, graceful Vienna School of football.

So to the Cup Final in Berne. Hungary, who had had to take a great deal more out of themselves than the Germans in their two previous matches, bowed to the insistence of Puskas and recalled him. This also meant the dropping of Budai, a very good outside-right, of whom Puskas for some reason did not approve.

Yet Hungary went quickly and efficiently into a 2–0 lead, which would have been enough to demoralize most teams. Germany, however, had great resources, and refused to give in. They scored once, twice and finally, through the burly Rahn – who had already got one of the goals – made the score 3–2, for victory. Puskas, who had missed a couple of good chances and was clearly not fully fit, streaked through late in the game to score what many thought a good equalizer. But the Welsh linesman, Mervyn Griffiths, stuck up his flag, to give him offside. Against all expectation, the World Cup was not Hungary's, but Germany's.

Though they played much attractive football in the World Cup of 1966, the days of Hungary's dominion were over. When the revolution broke out in Budapest in 1956, Honved chanced to be touring abroad. Puskas, Kocsis and Czibor never went home; they all, eventually, joined Spanish clubs: and that was effectively the end of a great team. So much for the belief that the Hungarians had found new, magical methods of training and playing. Like any other great team, their success depended basically on having a number of outstanding players who came forward together.

European Cup

In 1955, the first European Cup was played. A Cup competition for the League Champions of Europe, it was the idea of a veteran French football critic called Gabriel Hanot, who had played for France, managed the French national team for a while, and eventually died in 1968.

The birth of this tournament, played on a home-and-away, goal-aggregate pattern till the Final itself, marked a tremendous step forward in international football. Typically, the English League advised Chelsea, the English Champions, against taking part in the first tournament, but Manchester United, the new Champions, brushed their advice aside the following year. Fittingly, they would become the first English club to win the competition, in 1968.

In fact the European Cup was not the first competition of its kind, for the European Inter-Cities Fairs Cup, born as a long drawn-out tournament between teams which came from cities with an industrial fair, was already under way. In due course the European Cupwinners' Cup would follow, but the European Cup has remained far and away the most important of the three. Since 1960, the winners have met the winners of the South American Liberators' Cup, for the so-called intercontinental club championship.

Real Madrid

For the first five years, the European Cup was dominated by one great team and one great footballer. The team was Real Madrid, the unchallenged champions of Spain, the man an Argentinian centre-forward: Alfredo di Stefano.

Real were and are beyond doubt a fine club, but their success would have been impossible without the majestic and tireless Di Stefano, perhaps the most complete footballer of all time. Tall, blond and well built, he developed his amazing stamina by running through the streets of his native Buenos Aires. He was capable of having a shot at goal one minute, then popping up the next to tackle someone in his own penalty area. Other fine players came and went beside him; Raymond Kopa, the skilful little Frenchman, Gento, the quick left-winger, Ferenc Puskas, the Hungarian star. Others, such as the great Brazilian inside-forward, Didì, came to Madrid, kicked their heels for a season, and went home. Di Stefano made it quite clear that there was room for only one conductor on the podium.

The story goes that when Puskas first played in the team, the two of them were neck and neck for the honour of being leading goal-scorer in the Spanish Championship. In the last league match, Puskas found himself with an easy chance, but tactfully preferred to pass the ball to Di Stefano, who scored. From that moment, he was accepted.

Certainly the two worked beautifully together, as all who saw them share Real's seven goals against Eintracht in the European Final of 1960, at Hampden Park, will agree. Two years later, in Amsterdam, one remembers the astonishing pass with which Di Stefano sent Puskas through the helpless Benfica defence alone, to score; though Benfica, and Eusebio, were later to have the better of it, 5–3.

Di Stefano was one of the many Argentinian internationals who went to Bogota, Colombia, for the money. He stayed there, playing for Milonarios, for a number of years then, when Colombia rejoined FIFA and the golden bubble burst, went to Spain, where both Real and

Barcelona claimed him. The Spanish Federation, issuing a sort of Judgement of Solomon, ruled that Di Stefano should play for each club in alternating seasons; but Real managed to persuade Barcelona to sell their share in the Argentinian. Barcelona must often have regretted it.

It is sometimes forgotten that while English club football hovered on the brink, Hibernian gave it – and the Scottish Football Association – a lesson by entering the European Cup at once; and reaching the semi-final. The following season, the very good Manchester United team reached the semi-final round, too, before going down honourably and narrowly to Real Madrid. Even after the Munich crash, with their team in tatters, United gallantly achieved the semi-final again, not to mention the Final of the F.A. Cup. But alas, they lost in both, even though they did manage to defeat Milan, in Manchester. Eleven years later, Milan were to put them out in the semi-final again – and take away their Cup.

Helenio Herrera

Real's amazing monopoly came to an end at last in 1961, when Barcelona knocked them out; though Benfica of Lisbon, managed by a clever old Hungarian called Bela Guttmann, won the Final; then beat Real, as we have seen, in the next Final, too. Then it was the turn of the Italians; of Milan – who beat Benfica in the 1963 Final at Wembley – and of the other Milanese team, Internazionale, managed by the celebrated, flamboyant Helenio Herrera.

Brought up in the slums of Casablanca, in Morocco, the son of emigrants from Buenos Aires, Herrera became the most highly paid and publicized manager of his day. When he was in charge of Barcelona, he used to perform an almost religious ceremony with his players before each European Cup match. Each would have to place his hand solemnly on a football and cry, 'The European Cup, we *shall* have it, we *shall* have it!' and he would prepare them for the fray by getting them to jump about the gymnasium, shouting slogans. Slogans, indeed, have always been dear to him.

When he took over Internazionale, he at once festooned the dressing-room with placards: DEFENCE: LESS THAN THIRTY GOALS! ATTACK: MORE THAN 100 GOALS! 'Think of the match, think of next week's match!' he would cry to his sleepy team, as a motor coach drove them to an airport early in the morning after an away game. When Gerry Hitchens, the English international centre-forward who had a spell with Inter, left them in 1962, he remarked, 'It's like coming out of the Army!'

Catenaccio

With Barcelona, Herrera believed in attack, but when he found it would not work in Italy, he became more defensive than anybody. We were moving into the age of defensive, negative football, in which the Italian clubs, luring talent from all over the world, confined it in the prison of *catenaccio*.

Catenaccio means chain or bolt defence. It was supposedly invented by an Austrian coach, Karl Rappan, when he was in charge of the Swiss national team. It is strictly and horribly defensive, and its chief feature is that it uses a so-called 'sweeper-up' or 'sweeper', operating behind a line of four backs, and plugging whatever gaps may appear. A *catenaccio* formation looks like this:

Goal

Sweeper

Full Back   Centre Back   Centre Back   Full Back

Link-man   Link-man

Striker   Striker   Striker

You will see that there is a sweeper, four backs, two midfield players and three forwards, or strikers: but some *catenaccio* teams would play with three midfield men and only a miserable two strikers. In a three-striker attack, one of the three would be a straightforward winger, one probably an inside-forward of the goal-scoring kind, the other a centre-forward. In the 1970 European Cup Final the Dutch champions, Feyenoord, impressively showed how flexible the system can be, using it first to contain, then to overplay, Celtic.

The trouble with competitions such as the European Cup, with its two-legged ties, was that they encouraged such methods. If you avoided defeat away by defending in strength, you could hope to score enough goals at home to get through. But League football itself led directly to such methods. Since the away team is always at a natural disadvantage, it is equally and sadly natural that many an away team will play for a point; that's to say, concentrate on defence in the hope of getting a draw.

Not that Herrera's teams, at their best, were wholly defensive. They had a superb attacking full-back in the towering Giacinto Facchetti, who would come haring down the left wing in the space left by the absence of a true outside-left – and Jair, their Brazilian outside-right, was a splendid raider. But as Inter faded, they became increasingly defensive. Their victory over Real Madrid in the 1964 Final, though convincing, was one of grim efficiency over real football; even if Real were past their peak. And at last, in the European Final of 1967 in Lisbon, a now weary Inter were overwhelmed by a vigorously attacking Celtic team which became the first British side ever to win the competition.

Meanwhile, football was set on a course from which, alas, it has still to be diverted. The way was being prepared for the grim, negative football of the 1960s, even if, in 1958, the World Cup was won by one of the most attractive and talented teams ever to grace a football field.

7. Brazilian Samba

The Hungarians, who didn't win the World Cup, gave way to the Brazilians, who won it twice, and gave the game new tactics. In 1958, they won playing 4–2–4. In 1962, they won playing 4–3–3. Like the Gadarene swine plunging over that cliff, the football teams of the world rushed to imitate them, just as so many of them had rushed to imitate Arsenal and the third-back game in the 1930s; though the Italians stayed loyal to their wretched *catenaccio*. It took Feyenoord's display in Milan in 1970 to remind them it could be used for attack, as well as defence.

World Cup, 1958

For the only time so far in World Cup history, all four British teams took part in the 1958 finals. Wales were lucky; they had already been eliminated when, owing to withdrawals, the tournament needed one more team to play Israel. Various countries were invited to compete for the remaining place. Uruguay, surprisingly eliminated by Paraguay, proudly refused a second chance. Wales were not so proud: they beat Israel at home and away, to qualify.

Much more distinguished was the splendid performance of the Northern Ireland team, who actually beat and eliminated mighty Italy, in Belfast. Their team, admirably managed by Peter Doherty, one of the best inside-forwards Ireland had ever produced, now had a morale, a belief in itself it had never had when Doherty was a player. He had two fine lieutenants on and off the field in the clever, talented Danny Blanchflower and Jimmy McIlroy.

England's team, alas, was seriously affected by the death of Taylor, Byrne and, above all, Edwards, at Munich. Scotland had, if not an exceptional team, a much better one than in 1954, and would go out with some credit.

Brazil

The Brazilians, who were not especially well favoured when the competition began, had at long last prepared and organized with a determination which matched their players' gifts. Dr Hilton Gosling, the large, calm medical adviser who would play so great a part in winning two World Cups, had travelled the length and breadth of

Sweden before finding an ideal site for their training camp in Hindas, a well wooded area near Gothenburg. The new manager was the plump, Buddha-like figure, Vicente Feola, and the party even included a psychologist: though Feola didn't approve of the appointment. 'How can he know the scene?' he rumbled.

Though they began with a good-looking 3–0 win against the Austrians at Boraas, Brazil did not really get into their stride until the semi-finals. They were held to a draw by an England team strong in defence but dull in attack, where key players such as Johnny Haynes, Fulham's inside-left, and Bryan Douglas, Blackburn's outside-right, were showing the strain of a long struggle to come up with their clubs from the Second Division. Alas, Walter Winterbottom and his selectors would steadfastly refuse to make changes till the vital play-off against Russia: when two young forwards, Brabrook and Broadbent, were thrown in at the deep end for their first international.

Matters weren't helped by a severe injury to Tom Finney, the most gifted forward, in the opening match, drawn 2–2 against the Russians, a team whose defenders didn't stand on ceremony. Finney, who coolly scored the equalizer from the penalty spot, could not play another game in the series.

Wales and Ireland were, against all expectation, much the most successful and impressive of the four British teams. Partly this was because both of them achieved the happy, family atmosphere which England notoriously failed to create. So while England – though they did hold Brazil to that goalless draw – were plodding to eventual 1–0 defeat in their play-off with Russia ('Isn't it a sin and a shame that England should stay in the Park Avenue Hotel?' asked George Raynor, coaching Sweden), Wales and Ireland fought on to the quarter-finals. To do

95

this, Wales twice had to beat Hungary, while Ireland twice had to beat Czechoslovakia – once in the group qualifying match, once in a play-off, because they'd finished level on points. In each group, two teams went forward to the quarter-finals. Scotland, like England, didn't win a game, a draw with the Yugoslavs being the best they could manage.

Two survivors of the Manchester United team which crashed at Munich attended this World Cup. Harry Gregg, the big Irish goalkeeper who had bravely dragged people clear of the burning wreckage, had an outstanding game for Ireland against Germany. Bobby Charlton, only nineteen years old, didn't get a game for England, despite a fierce newspaper campaign in his favour.

Perhaps it was as well for Charlton, still seriously affected by the shock of the crash, that he was not thrust into the team, when so much would have been expected of him. His time would come.

After drawing with England, a deputation of Brazilian players asked that Garrincha, the Botafogo outside-right, be chosen for their third game, against Russia. A mulatto, who had been been born with a leg so seriously deformed that it required an operation, and was still notably bent, Garrincha was already known for his brilliance and inconsistency. But the players had their way. He was chosen against Russia, exploited his marvellous acceleration and astonishing swerve 'outside' the full-back through the first half, and helped his team to win 2–0.

The 4–2–4 formation they were playing looked like this:

Goal
(Gilmar)

Full Back   1st Centre Half   2nd Centre Half   Full Back
(D.Santos)   (Bellini)   (Orlando)   (N. Santos)

Link-man   Link-man
(Zito)   (Didi)

Outside Right   Striker   Striker   Outside Left
(Garrincha)   (Vava)   (Pelé)   (Zagalo)

There were, you will see, two centre-backs, two mid-field, constructive players, and four strikers: two wingers and two men in the middle. What all this meant, in effect, was that a regular stopper centre-half and a defensive wing-half played in the middle of the defence (Bellini and Orlando), a constructive, attacking wing-half and inside-forward (Zito and Didì) were the two men in mid-field, while two wingers (Garrincha and Zagalo), a centre-forward (Vavà) and a striking inside-forward (Pelé) operated in front.

The system, which had first been used in Rio club football by a Paraguayan coach, Fleitas Solich, had this advantage; it sealed up the defensive middle, where the

Brazilians had been notoriously unable to master the covering of the third-back game. The wholly defensive wing-half, playing beside the centre-half, had existed for some time : Hungary had used him, in the shape of Zakarias.

Otherwise, the Brazilian system, like any other, tended to depend on the quality of players available. Just as Arsenal, in the 1930s, had found an Alex James, so Brazil had the perfect midfield couple of the elegant Zito and the clever Didì. In attack, Vavà was tremendously active and thrustful, Zagalo had two men's stamina, Garrincha on his day was irresistible, while the seventeen-year-old Pelé was a new and exciting figure, as cool and mature as he was greatly gifted.

Born into a poor Negro family in the State of Minas Gerais, he had been a Santos club player and an international since he was sixteen; strong, wonderfully gymnastic, strong in the air – and with a fine right foot.

Yet Wales, even though they lacked their chief star, the big centre-forward, John Charles, put up a masterly defence against Brazil in the quarter-finals at Gothenburg, and fell only to a rather lucky, late goal by Pelé, deflected past the excellent Jack Kelsey. (A goalkeeper who explained his safe handling: 'Chewinggum. Always use it. Put some on my hands. Rub it well in.')

Ireland, tired after an unnecessarily long coach journey, and seriously affected by injuries, fell 4–0 to a French team in which the deadly partnership of Raymond Kopa, making the bullets, and Just Fontaine, firing them, had brought unexpected progress. Sweden, meanwhile, beat Russia in the quarter-finals, their team including Gren and Liedholm, of the 1948 team, Skoglund, now a left-winger, of the 1949 team, and a spectacular new right-winger in Kurt Hamrin. The fact that professionals were now at last allowed to play in Swedish football permitted Raynor to use such 'exiles'.

It was interesting to see how the Swedes, at first dour and pessimistic, suddenly came to life as their unfancied team made progress. By the semi-finals Gothenburg was a cauldron of patriotism; so much so that the Swedes fell foul of FIFA by actually putting their cheer leaders on the field before the match. They beat West Germany 3–1 in an exciting, sometimes violent game. The Brazilians, helped by an injury to the polished French centre-half, Bob Jonquet, beat France 5–2 in the other semi-final.

Raynor seemed confident Sweden would win the Final, in Stockholm. 'If the Brazilians give away an early goal, they panic all over the show,' he said. Brazil did give away an early goal, when Liedholm picked his way as sure and calm as a chamois through their defence; but they did not panic. Instead, Garrincha's two astonishing runs down the right and fast, low crosses gave Vavà two goals, to turn the game before half-time. Later, Pelé scored twice, once with his head, once, after some incredibly cool juggling, with his foot, and Zagalo once, against one more by Sweden's Simonsson.

'Samba, samba!' cried the Brazilians in the crowd; and when the game was over and their happy tears had been shed, Brazil's players trotted round the pitch, carrying the Swedish flag.

World Cup, 1962

In 1962, they won again, succeeding in the extraordinary gamble of fielding almost exactly the same side; though now it played 4–3–3. Or rather, it did so after Pelé, regarded as the key man, had pulled a muscle severely in his second game, in the beautiful little stadium of Viña del Mar, on the coast of Chile.

Amarildo, a twenty-four-year-old reserve player, successfully took his place, and the tireless left-winger Zagalo, began to play a deeper-lying game. In this respect he may be compared with Hidegkuti in the old Hungarian side, for he had the same ability to play a midfield or a striker's game, as the situation allowed. 4–3–3, which was as eagerly imitated by the world at large – less Italy – as 4–2–4 had been, after 1958, and was England's method in 1966, followed this pattern:

Goal

Full Back   1st Centre Half   2nd Centre Half   Full Back

Link-man   Link-man   Link-man

Striker   Striker   Striker

Generally speaking, *one* of the three so-called *front runners* is a normal winger, doing his work out on the flank; but when England won the World Cup in 1966, they did so without a recognized winger in the team.

The England team of 1962 did modestly well. Staying away up in the mountains, at Coya, it came down to play its qualifying matches in the little copper company stadium at Rancagua, losing 2–1 to Hungary, winning 3–1 against Argentina and drawing 0–0 with the Bulgarians. Bobby Charlton, playing as a left winger, moved and shot beautifully, his right foot now the equal of a naturally powerful left, and a new left-half, the tall, blond Bobby Moore, was another success.

The team as a whole, however, pivoting in midfield on Johnny Haynes, lacked surprise. Opponents usually knew what it, and Haynes, was going to do, and Brazil, with Garrincha in unstoppable form, defeated them 3–1 in the quarter-final at Viña. No other British team had qualified.

Brazil weren't the force they had been in Sweden, but Garrincha's marvellous shooting and jumping – he headed superb goals against England and, in the semi-final, Chile – took them through to the Final.

Czechoslovakia, who had already drawn with the Brazilians in their qualifying group at Viña, were the other finalists; appearing in a World Cup Final for the second time since 1934. They had a clever if rather slow team, well served in midfield by Josef Masopust, the left-half, and Kvasniak, a lanky inside-forward.

Masopust it was who actually scored the first goal of the game, in Santiago, when Scherer put him through Brazil's defence, but alas for the Czechs, their goalkeeper, Josef Schroiff, previously their hero, was to have a poor day.

Before half-time, Amarildo beat him from an 'impos-

8. The British Revival

In July, 1966, England at last won the World Cup. In May, 1967, Celtic won the European Cup. A year later, Manchester United won it. At long last, after years of struggle and disappointment, the great trophies were falling to British teams. What had happened?

Broadly, that foreign methods and ideas, having finally been understood and properly appreciated in our football, had been absorbed and blended with our own natural talents, to form a potent combination. This blending was due in part to the effects of the Football Association Coaching Scheme, and the good coaches it had produced (it has produced a number of less good ones, too, hiding behind a cloud of technical terms), in part to the emergence of some fine manager-coaches.

Ramsey and Stein

Sir Alf Ramsey and Jock Stein were and are among the best of these, though neither ever took an F.A. coaching

103

course. Ramsey, after his distinguished playing years with Spurs and England, became manager of little Ipswich Town, took them from the Third to the First Division and, with a team of largely 'unknown' and several elderly players, actually won the Championship. In 1963 this quiet, shy, loyal, determined man took over the England team, won the admiration of his players, introduced new tactics, and at length kept the promise he made when he took office: 'We shall win the World Cup.'

In Scotland, Jock Stein, who had been an unexceptional centre-half with Albion Rovers, was recalled to his own country by Celtic, when he was playing in the Southern League for Llanelly, led a revival in which he skippered them to Cup and League – breaking the monopoly of Rangers – and, after managing Dunfermline and Hibernian, returned to Celtic as manager. The team he built, with an emphasis on ball training, speed and *attack* in an era of defence, became the first from Britain to win the European Cup.

Ramsey moved patiently towards his goal. He was precise as a sergeant-major in speech, always putting his players first – he threatened to resign when officials wanted him to drop Nobby Stiles, after incidents in the 1966 World Cup. The fact that the World Cup would take place in England was a huge help; though England's dreary performances at Wembley in the eliminating rounds, against Uruguay, Mexico and France, were scarcely encouraging.

Believing at first in the importance of wingers to 'turn' a packed defence – taking the ball to the goal-line before crossing it – Ramsey decided on a 'wingless' policy after these early matches, because the wingers he wanted weren't there. Funnily enough, however, a superb performance *on* the right wing by the little, piping-voiced, red-haired Alan Ball, helped more than any other single factor to win the World Cup Final.

World Cup, 1966

England did not play well in the quarter-final, either, against Argentina, who did their best to spoil it as a game of football. A host of deliberate fouls resulted, at last, in their captain, the tall Antonio Rattin, being sent off; and some very unpleasant scenes. Argentina, alas, had been so badly shaken by a 6–1 defeat at the hands of the Czechs in the 1958 World Cup, followed by a pelting with rubbish by fans at Buenos Aires airport, that they had given up their old, artistic play for toughness. This ruthless approach to football would give them the world championship for clubs in 1967 and 1968, after scandalously rough matches against Celtic and Manchester United. But in 1966, it was a sad waste of the talents of such players as Artime and Onega, in attack: and Rattin.

Even against ten men, England's uninspired attack made very heavy weather of its task, but at last Geoff Hurst, who had been brought into the attack in preference to the famous Tottenham goal-scorer, Jimmy Greaves, jumped beautifully to head the winner. He would stay – to score a record three goals in the Final, and develop into one of the most courageous and dangerous strikers of his day. Yet only a few weeks earlier, on tour in Copenhagen, he had played so poorly for England against Denmark that his international career seemed over.

The most exciting quarter-final was unquestionably that between Portugal and the 'unknown' North Koreans. The Asian team, who had had to beat only Australia to qualify, were a completely unknown quantity when they arrived to play their matches in Middlesbrough; though it *was* known that they were all army officers whose lives were dedicated to football, under a military discipline.

So quickly did they improve that in their third match they actually beat Italy, with a goal by Pak Doo Ik. Then, in the quarter-final at Everton, they quickly went into a 3–0 lead against the Portuguese team which had previously beaten Brazil, mistakenly faithful to their stars of 1962 and 1958.

Luckily for Portugal, their lithe, coloured inside-right, Eusebio, from Mozambique, took over the game at that point, enabling his team to win 5–3. In the semi-final, however, Portugal faced an England team at last moving smoothly and thrustfully, worth much more than the 2–1 win it achieved, thanks to two splendid goals by Bobby Charlton. Playing now as a 'deep' centre-forward, Bobby had his older brother, the tall Jackie, behind him, at centre-half.

West Germany were England's opponents in the Final, and a fine, open, exciting game it was. Germany took the lead when Ray Wilson, the England left-back, untypically nodded a cross straight to the German inside-right, Haller. Hurst headed the equalizer from Moore's free-kick. Martin Peters, Hurst's clever colleague at West Ham, made it 2–1 in the second half, after a corner; but just on time, Weber stole up to equalize after a free kick doubtfully given against Jackie Charlton; and England had to begin all over again : as Alf Ramsey told them.

With Alan Ball running like a racehorse, they did. He made another goal for Hurst – confirmed by the Russian linesman when the ball bounced down from the bar – and finally, near the last whistle, Hurst ran through a tired, scattered German defence to get the fourth with a smashing, left-footed shot.

European Cup

The following year, Jock Stein's boundlessly energetic
Celtic team fought back gloriously from an early penalty
goal against them, in Lisbon, to outplay Inter in the
European Final. Their spectacular equalizing goal was
scored by their attacking left-back, Tommy Gemmell.

Then, after so many disappointments in the semi-final,
it was Manchester United's turn at Wembley, a superb
individual goal at the start of extra time by Ireland's
little George Best turning the Final against Benfica.
Best, the most popular, publicized and generally attractive British footballer of his day – perhaps of any day –
spun like a possessed humming top past one man, walked
round the goalkeeper, and calmly shot home.

With his flapping 'Beatle' locks, his appeal to the
young, his gay life off the field, Best stood for the new
kind of footballer, made possible by the abolition of the
maximum wage. And in his electric skills and daring, he
showed that there is still room, even among today's
packed, tough defences, for the individual star.

Violence

The combination, however, of increasingly international,
and increasingly lucrative, competition among the clubs,
has made the life of a Best or a Pelé harder and harder.
Best, both in the European Final of 1968 and the shame-
ful world club championship matches of the same year –
against Estudiantes de la Plata of Argentina – was dis-
gracefully ill-treated by opponents. Though the star
British player, who till the abolition of the maximum
wage in 1961 could earn only £20 a week, may now earn
between £5,000 and £10,000 a year, it is often at a heavy
physical price.

The distressing incidents which took place in the Estudiantes–Manchester United game in Buenos Aires – Charlton was viciously kicked, Stiles brutally headed in the face, while in Manchester, Best was provoked and then sent off when he retaliated – had already been exceeded by what happened the previous year, when Celtic played Racing Club of Buenos Aires. The deciding match, in Montevideo, ended in a fearsome brawl, Celtic's players having at last been provoked beyond restraint. In Buenos Aires, Simpson, their goalkeeper, had been hit on the head by a stone, catapulted from the crowd, and put out of the game, before a ball was kicked.

In 1969, the pot finally boiled over. The cynical ruthlessness of Argentinian football resulted in a hair-raising world club championship return match between Estudiantes and Milan in Buenos Aires. Aguirre Suarez, one of the Argentinian stoppers, deliberately smashed his elbow into the face of Nestor Combin, Milan's Argentinian centre-forward, breaking his nose. He and another Estudiantes player, Manera, were sent off the field.

On this occasion, however, General Ongania, Argentina's military dictator, intervened, ordering both these players and Poletti, the goalkeeper, to be first imprisoned, then suspended. Poletti was disqualified for life, while the other two were given long sentences.

The grim question arose of whether football could continue to be played in such conditions. People may laugh, today, at the old Corinthian spirit of sportsmanship, but it had, and has, its practical side. Any sport involving body-contact must depend on restraint by both sides. There is nothing easier than for an ill-intentioned team to make the game unplayable. When that happens, football becomes an impossibility, however strong the referees, however severe the punishment visited on offenders. A hopeful sign for the future was Argentina's elimination in 1969 from the World Cup tournament by a Peruvian team which played joyfully attacking football – with *two* wingers. But there was much concern on the eve of the 1970 World Cup in which England alone survived, to represent British football.

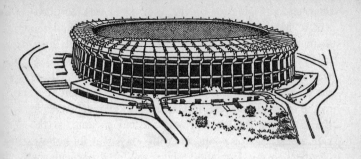

9. World Cup, 1970

The 1970 World Cup was won triumphantly, convincingly and excitingly by a Brazilian team which gave new hope to football. New hope, because they won by sheer skill, sheer excellence in attacking play. Indeed, they cast happy doubt on the whole defensive idea of soccer which had gradually been strangling the game in its embrace. Brazil, in fact, had a quite mediocre defence and, in Felix, probably the worst goalkeeper ever to win a World Cup medal. Yet in the Final, when they came up against Italy, the very ach-priests of defensive football, the exponents of the *catenaccio* game, they overwhelmed them, winning 4–1.

The World Cup was held, though it should not have been, in Mexico. There was, in the first place, a serious problem of altitude. Most of the cities in which World Cup matches were played stand many thousands of feet above sea level. Players, like our own, who are used to playing at sea level need several weeks to get used to the thin air. If they try to play after only a few days, they find themselves gasping for breath. Worse still was the problem of heat. It would have been all very well had the matches been played, as they should logically have been, in the evening, when it was cooler. But because they wanted huge sums of money from European television, the organizers of the World Cup, giving no thought at all to the unhappy players, forced them to kick off either in the afternoon or, when it was a Sunday game, at the ridiculous hour of noon, when the day is at its hottest. Needless to say, England's players suffered particularly. Yet, although they were eliminated in the quarter-finals, it was not unfair to call them one of the best teams in the competition. Many foreign journalists thought they were most unlucky not to reach the Final. Had they done so, they would surely have put up a much better fight than Italy, who were lucky to come back into the game at all, thanks to a very simple and silly error by the otherwise excellent Clodoaldo.

But let us look at this fine and sometimes dazzling Brazilian team, and its stars. Above all, as we know, they had Pelé, now playing in his fourth World Cup, and playing as wonderfully as ever. 'I'll never forget that,' said Alan Ball, England's midfield player, of the extraordinary lob from the very centre circle, with which Pelé almost scored a goal against an astounded Czech goalkeeper, in the opening match. In the Final, he was perhaps not at his most spectacular, and was somewhat eclipsed by the superb performance of Gerson, in midfield. Yet what can one say of a man who still manages to score a splendid first goal with his head, leaping like a cat, and to lay on two for other players?

Gerson, who did not play against England because he was injured, was a magnificent midfield player, using his powerful and amazingly accurate left foot beautifully. It should be explained that one of the effects of the thin air in Mexico is that the ball meets less resistance and therefore travels farther and faster. The Brazilians, who are especially good at making use of free kicks – Pelé, Gerson and Rivelino, whose own left foot is formidably strong, were the experts – exploited this with great success. The goal with which Gerson restored Brazil's lead, midway through the second half of the final, was memorable indeed. He turned on the ball outside the penalty area, and hit a ferocious low shot into the opposite corner. One can think of few other players who could have done it; though Rivelino is certainly one. The other goals for Brazil were scored by their big, fast, powerful outside-right, Jairzinho, and, last of all, by their captain, Carlos Alberto, racing through down the right flank into abundant open space, as he had done so often before in the game.

Italy beat Mexico very comfortably 4–1 in the quarter-finals, and won a thrilling and remarkable semi-final against West Germany 4–3 in extra time, when the Germans tired, but they were really somewhat lucky to go as far as the Final. Their performance in the qualifying group, at Puebla and Toluca, was cautious and boring in the extreme. They all seemed to be perfectly terrified of another humiliating defeat such as North Korea inflicted on them in 1966 at Middlesbrough. So they scraped through by the skin of their teeth against Sweden, scoring the only goal, and drew drearily not only with Uruguay (badly hampered by injury to their star inside-forward, Pedro Rocha), but even with little Israel.

Of the 'minnows' who took part in the competition, Israel and Morocco were much the most surprising and best. The Moroccans, in their opening game, gave the West Germans a terrible fright, scoring the first goal and holding out well into the second half, when the Germans

– for whom the splendid Uwe Seeler was also playing in his fourth World Cup – popped in two goals.

Rather surprisingly, Uruguay and Italy, qualifying from this tedious Group II, both won their quarter-final matches. The Uruguayans, big, heavy men with surprisingly delicate ball control, took the Russians to extra time in the mighty Azteca Stadium, in Mexico City, then won with a late and very contentious goal, after the ball seemed to have gone out of play. They then met Brazil, in Guadalajara, an old, familiar enemy whom they'd surprised very often in the past and shocked again, when weird goalkeeping by Felix allowed Cubilla to score. But Brazil then exerted all their manifold arts and crafts. Clodoaldo equalized, Jairzinho and Rivelino put in two more.

Uruguay lost the third-place match to a very tired West German team which scored a glorious early goal through another of its finest players, Wolfgang Overath (Beckenbauer, injured against Italy, missed the game; he played throughout extra time in the semi-final with his arm strapped to his chest). After that it was mostly Uruguay, but they missed chance after chance and simply couldn't get the ball in the net. Nevertheless, they had again proved how remarkably their team always responds to the challenge of a World Cup.

England, though they lost two matches and with them their title, certainly did not disgrace themselves, and if the luck had run a little more kindly for them, would probably have reached the Final. So many things were against them that it was always unlikely that they would keep the Cup. For one thing, they were drawn in Group III in Guadalajara, much the most difficult group of all four. Whereas in every other group there was at least one weak team, so that the stronger teams in the group had, so to speak, a day off each, England were obliged to play against three powerful opponents: the Rumanians, the Brazilians and Czechs.

There were other hardships, too; above all, that of heat. When England played and lost to Brazil in a marvellously thrilling game at the Jalisco Stadium, the temperature rose as high as 98 degrees. When you remember that a day when it rises to 75 degrees is considered unusually hot and trying in England, you can imagine how hard it must have been for the English players. It was amazing that most of them lasted so well, although in almost every case they lost more than ten pounds in weight.

The high altitude was, of course, another great problem, though England were able to prepare for this, leaving home nearly a month before their first World Cup match. Guadalajara, besides, was not so high as Mexico City, being rather over 5,000 feet, where Mexico City stands more than 7,000 feet.

England played well to beat Rumania in their opening match, which they won with a goal powerfully shot with his left foot by Geoff Hurst. This was rather fitting, as it was the same player and exactly the same foot which had scored England's last World Cup goal, against West Germany, at Wembley.

Then came the Brazil match, and some unexpected, thoroughly unpleasant troubles. For one reason and another, the touchy and thin-skinned Mexican public had decided the English had snubbed them. So the night before the game, while the English players were trying to sleep in the Hilton Hotel, they paraded outside with cars and motor bikes, honking horns and generally making an atrocious din, cheering for Brazil, and deliberately trying to stop the English players sleeping. The appalling noise went on into the small hours of the morning, for the police, although appeals were made to them, stayed away from the hotel and did nothing. Several of the players had to change their rooms, and move on to the other side of the hotel.

Thus the players, many of whom had been very tense and nervous before the Rumanian game – 'I've never been so terrified in my life,' confessed Alan Ball – were faced with another hazard.

In the circumstances, the game against Brazil was a marvellous one. If England had only taken the three or four excellent chances which fell to them, they might have won. As it was, the Brazilians, who played some beautiful football in attack, won with a fine goal in the second half, when Tostao survived three tackles on the left, crossed the ball, and the marvellous Pelé deftly pushed it to Jairzinho, who came racing in to score. Even Gordon Banks, who had made an astounding one-handed save from Pelé's header in the first half (Pelé was already shouting, 'Goal! '), could do nothing about it.

Bobby Moore, the English captain and left-half, had a superb match, dominating play with majestic assurance. It was hard to believe that, only a couple of weeks before, he had been involved in a distressing incident in Bogota, Colombia, where he had been outrageously accused of stealing a bracelet. Luckily for England, he was allowed out of Colombia after a few days, and the charges against him were laughed to scorn all over the world.

England played badly against the Czechs, scraping through 1–0 with a penalty kick coolly taken by Allan Clarke, one of several reserves who came in for the match. Once again the Mexican crowd was bitterly against them from the beginning, whistling and jeering them throughout the game.

So England finished second in their group, and had to travel to the higher, more humid and almost equally hot city of Leon, to play the West Germans: a 'revenge' for the World Cup Final of 1966.

It might be said, with some justice, that a bottle of beer cost England the game. The beer was drunk by their splendid goalkeeper, Gordon Banks, who was taken ill later that Saturday. He was put to bed with a high temperature while the doctor and the team hoped against hope that he would recover in time. Next morning, in the grounds of the Estancia Motel, where England stayed, you could see Banks and the doctor walking slowly together. Alas, he was not fit, and Peter Bonetti had to take his place, after weeks without a competitive game.

Though England took a well-deserved 2–0 lead, through Alan Mullery and Martin Peters – both goals coming from perfect centres by the overlapping right-back, Keith Newton – Germany recovered to get three, the winner being scored by the formidable Gerd Muller in extra time. Most people thought that Banks would at least have saved the long shot with which Franz Beckenbauer, a wonderfully fluent, elegant half-back, made it 2–1 and re-opened the game. Many thought he would also have saved Uwe Seeler's header, and have cut out the crosses which preceded Muller's goal.

The truth is, however, that England became very tired, and Terry Cooper, who had done wonderfully well in the first match against Rumania and had played Libuda out of the game in Leon, was eventually given a tremendous chasing by the substitute, Grabowski.

Some blamed Sir Alf Ramsey for substituting Bobby Charlton, playing in his 106th game and thus beating Billy Wright's record, and Martin Peters with Colin Bell and Norman Hunter. Others felt that his 4–4–2 system was too negative and inflexible. I certainly agreed with those who thought that the World Cup of 1970 demonstrated the tremendous importance of wingers, in whom Ramsey doesn't believe. Such players as Jairzinho,

117

Postscript

The season which followed the 1970 World Cup was, overall, an immense disappointment. Where Brazil had so shiningly and triumphantly led the way, nobody followed. Where Brazil had shown that attack could still be the best form of defence – indeed, had made it compensate for a weak defence! – that skill and technique could still win the highest prizes, the game at large sluggishly refused to take risks.

England, under the rigid, cautious managership of Sir Alf Ramsey, lost not a single match, but continued to play dull, unadventurous football, above all in the International Championship, when only a very lucky goal achieved victory in Belfast, Wales forced a goalless draw at Wembley, and success came only in the last match, against a feeble Scottish side.

Arsenal emulated Tottenham Hotspur by becoming the second English team this century to win the League and Cup double, that double which had eluded all their great, exciting sides between the wars. But though their achievement was extraordinary, the manner of it was prosaic and leaden, the product of sheer, grinding persistence, rather than flair. In their last six home matches, five were arduously won by a 1–0 margin. There were many gifted players in the side, not least the long-haired Charlie George, a locally born inside-forward who scored the winning goal in the Cup Final. But, by and large, the watchword was caution. Exuberance was the last quality one would associate with Arsenal's triumph, or with their belief in 'work rate'; as if work alone can compensate for skill and flair.

It was especially sad, and significant, that both Arsenal and England should use a converted full-back, Peter Storey, as a midfield player, a position in which ball control and imagination are so important. Ruthless in the tackle and capable, from time to time, of getting important goals, Storey was certainly an effective footballer, but his use by Arsenal was a sign that they wanted to hedge their bets, to have it both ways; and when Ramsey picked him in the same role for England, it was a still clearer sign of the unadventurousness of his policies.

Perhaps it was the European Cup Final, above all, which displayed how little effect Brazil's success had had on the European, not to say the world, game. Ajax, the highly talented Dutch team which won the trophy, playing their second Final in three years, were, like the Brazilians, endowed with a brilliant attack and a flimsy defence. In Johan Cruyff, their long-haired, long-legged centre-forward, they had one of the game's outstanding players, a superb individualist with glorious control and acceleration. They were opposed in the Wembley Final by Panathinaikos, a Greek team which, to general amazement, had defeated Everton and Red Star Belgrade to reach the Final; they were under the managership of Ferenc Puskas, the former Hungarian star.

Both individually and collectively, it was plain that the Greeks couldn't hope to match Ajax, who scored after only five minutes to kill Greek hopes of playing a successful defensive game. Time and again, using the great, open spaces of Wembley, Cruyff and company tore open the Greek defence. But by half-time they had not scored again, and in the second half, they shut up shop, played defensively themselves, and scored only one late goal from a rather lucky deflection. In other words, their approach was exactly the reverse of Brazil's in Mexico.

Nevertheless, the rise of Dutch football, which had now won the European Cup for two successive years, was a fine reality. English clubs won the other two European trophies. Chelsea, making light of many injuries, eventually beat Real Madrid in a replayed Cupwinners' Cup Final in Athens, in which Charlie Cooke, their brilliant Scottish international inside-forward, expressed the full range of his talents. Leeds United, similarly beset all season by injury, won the last of the European Fairs Cups on 'away' goals, against Juventus of Turin. From 1971–2, the European Union Cup would take its place.

Yet perhaps the most important feature of the British season was the sudden rise of a crop of young graduates in First Division football. The most spectacular and successful of them was a twenty-two-year-old Irish International centre-forward, Steve Heighway, who had only just turned professional with Liverpool at a ripe 'old' age. Brian Hall, in Liverpool's midfield, was another, Blackpool had the twenty-two-year-old Oxford Blue, Peter Suddaby, while Manchester United had Alan Gowling, another B.Sc. in economics.

What it meant, apart from the fact that the high rewards of football were attracting a better-educated class of player, was that a myth had been exploded. Quite clearly you do *not* have to turn professional at fifteen, do *not* have to dedicate your whole life to the game from boyhood, thus throwing away your chances of a decent education, and gambling dangerously on your footballing talents.

This was the more reassuring, and the more ironical, in the very season that Liverpool's chief scout in Wales announced that he had been told to look for players nine years old and *under*!

It was to be hoped that Steve Heighway's example would encourage intelligent boys, and their parents, not to throw away the chance of a good education, but to pursue it as far as they could, knowing that they might still succeed as footballers.

Another fact which became depressingly clear was that our professionals were being obliged to play far too much football. The season was too long and competitions often overlapped one another in the most alarming way. When Alan Mullery, the right-half and captain of Tottenham Hotspur, withdrew from the England team to play for the British title in May, on the grounds of exhaustion, the writing was on the wall.

The chaos in April 1971, when fixtures in the European Nations Cup and the three Major European club competitions virtually fell over one another, was ridiculous. Wales, in the Nations Cup, had to put out a skeleton team against the Czechs, and lost. Greece 'solved' the problem by not picking a single player from Panathinaikos, then so deeply involved in the European Cup, against England and Switzerland!

Then, at the very end of May, came an ill-conceived Anglo-Italian tournament which fairly put the lid on things. With players such as Arsenal's being obliged to play more than sixty fully competitive matches a season, it was obvious that something would have to be done; and quickly.

The following season, a sinister outcrop of injuries to the pelvic girdle muscle among our footballers emphasized the seriousness of the problem.

It was not a happy season for Sir Alf Ramsey and England, thoroughly beaten 3–1 at Wembley in the quarter-final of the European Nations Cup. While the German team, and Ajax, who retained the European Cup, had developed a splendidly flexible new method, known as 'total football', Ramsey's tactics looked rigid and old-fashioned. The Dutch and Germans showed encouragingly that *catenaccio* tactics, provided you had a brilliantly versatile sweeper like Beckenbauer, need not be defensive and negative as they remained in Italy.

So much was demonstrated in the European final when Ajax, playing the 'new *catenaccio*', overwhelmed Inter playing the old, cautious kind.

The West Germans employed a new, 'total football' much more devastatingly in the European Nations Cup, thrashing England at Wembley in the quarter-final, brushing aside the Russians in the final in Brussels. It was a great triumph for their manager, Helmut Schoen, and seemed to have revolutionized the whole, once muscular, nature of German football.

Table of Results

WORLD CUP WINNERS

	Winners	Venue
1930	Uruguay	Montevideo
1934	Italy	Rome
1938	Italy	Paris
1950	Uruguay	Rio
1954	West Germany	Berne
1958	Brazil	Stockholm
1962	Brazil	Santiago
1966	England	London
1970	Brazil	Mexico City

WORLD CLUB CHAMPIONS

	Winners	Runners-up
1960	Real Madrid	Penarol
1961	Penarol	Benfica
1962	Santos	Benfica
1963	Santos	Milan
1964	Internazionale	Independiente
1965	Internazionale	Independiente
1966	Penarol	Real Madrid
1967	Racing Club	Celtic
1968	Estudiantes	Manchester United
1969	Milan	Estudiantes
1970	Feyenoord	Estudiantes
1971	Nacional	Panathinaikos
1972	Ajax	Independiente

EUROPEAN CUP WINNERS

	Winners	*Runners-up*
1956	Real Madrid	Reims
1957	Real Madrid	Fiorentina
1958	Real Madrid	Milan
1959	Real Madrid	Reims
1960	Real Madrid	Eintracht
1961	Benfica	Barcelona
1962	Benfica	Real Madrid
1963	Milan	Benfica
1964	Internazionale	Real Madrid
1965	Internazionale	Benfica
1966	Real Madrid	Partizan
1967	Celtic	Internazionale
1968	Manchester United	Benfica
1969	Milan	Ajax Amsterdam
1970	Feyenoord	Celtic
1971	Ajax	Panathinaikos
1972	Ajax	Internazionale
1973	Ajax	Juventus

EUROPEAN CUP-WINNERS' CUP

	Winners	*Runners-up*
1961	Fiorentina	Rangers
1962	Atletico Madrid	Fiorentina
1963	Tottenham Hotspur	Atletico Madrid
1964	Sporting Lisbon	MTK Budapest
1965	West Ham United	Munich 1860
1966	Borussia Dortmund	Liverpool
1967	Bayern Munich	Rangers
1968	Milan	S.V. Hamburg
1969	Slovan Bratislava	Barcelona
1970	Manchester City	Gornik
1971	Chelsea	Real Madrid

1972	Rangers	Moscow Dynamo
		(Dynamo lodged a protest)
1973	Milan	Leeds United

EUROPEAN FAIRS CUP

	Winners	*Runners-up*
1958	Barcelona	London
1960	Barcelona	Birmingham City
1961	Roma	Birmingham City
1962	Valencia	Barcelona
1963	Valencia	Dynamo Zagreb
1964	Saragossa	Valencia
1965	Ferencvaros	Juventus
1966	Barcelona	Saragossa
1967	Dynamo Zagreb	Leeds United
1968	Leeds United	Ferencvaros
1969	Newcastle United	Ujpest
1970	Arsenal	Anderlecht
1971	Leeds United	Juventus

In 1971, the competition became the European Union
(U.E.F.A.) Cup.

	Winners	*Runners-up*
1972	Tottenham Hotspur	Wolverhampton Wanderers
1973	Liverpool	Borussia Munchengladbach

EUROPEAN (NATIONS CUP) CHAMPIONSHIP

	Winners	*Runners-up*	*Venue*
1960	Russia	Yugoslavia	Paris
1964	Spain	Russia	Madrid
1968	Italy	Yugoslavia	Rome

EUROPEAN FOOTBALLER OF THE YEAR

		Nationality
1956	Stanley Matthews	England
1957	Alfredo Di Stefano	Spain
1958	Raymond Kopa	France
1959	Alfredo Di Stefano	Spain
1960	Luis Suarez	Spain
1961	Omar Sivori	Italy
1962	Josef Masopust	Czechoslovakia
1963	Lev Yachine	Russia
1964	Denis Law	Scotland
1965	Eusebio	Portugal
1966	Bobby Charlton	England
1967	Florian Albert	Hungary
1968	George Best	Northern Ireland
1969	Gianni Rivera	Italy
1970	Gerd Muller	West Germany
1971	Johan Cruyff	Holland
1972	Franz Beckenbauer	West Germany

If you have enjoyed this book and would like
to know about others which we publish, why not
join the Puffin Club? You will be sent the Club
magazine *Puffin Post* four times a year and a
smart badge and membership book. You will
also be able to enter all the competitions. For
details, send a stamped addressed envelope to:

The Puffin Club, Dept A
Penguin Books
Bath Road
Harmondsworth
Middlesex